Advance Praise for
Bengt O Björklund's

⦚⦚⦚ I0165458

"Bengt's poetry and sensitivity touches me now as it did back in Turkish prison in 1970. The character of Erich in my book Midnight Express is partly based upon him, and while my sexual relationship [as portrayed in the movie] was [actually] with another prisoner, it was Bengt's smiling soul that helped transform the concrete walls and prison bars . . . his writing is clean, no punctuation, just words and the dreams lingering behind them. When I read: "a dream birthed me in eastern jail austerity" I remember those days and wish my old friend well."

—Billy Hayes,
author of *Midnight Express*

"This uncensored collection from Middle Creek Publishing is a testament to Björklund's abundance of poetic output, the collection acts almost, as a running commentary upon a personal exercise in Björklund's creative practice. The exercise is a profound interrogation of the meaning and position of the word "I.""

find me not in disarray
where I river blind survive
where the silent I can play
find me not so unkind and alive

The reader is invited into the poems through an empathy with the eponymous "I," who is both lost and full of self-doubt but, of course, singularly all-consuming. The poet is always seeking new experience and constantly finding beauty in all he encounters. While identifying with the futility of an attempt to relive all of human experience, the unavoidable strength of connection achieved by the relentless repetition of such a singular and uniquely powerful letter in the English language forces the reader to examine their own relationship with mortality, society and self.

Dylan Thomas is one of the greatest influences upon Björklund, and 45 years after his forced incarceration where he first encountered the works of Dylan Thomas, Bjorklund finds himself, perhaps, imprisoned again by his "craft or sullen art." For me, the spirit of "I" is summed up in these lines of Dylan Thomas from his poem "Fern Hill"

'Oh as I was young and easy in the mercy of his means,
Time held me green and dying' "

— Dominic Williams,
poet, editor of *Carmarthen* and *A Map of Love*

Bengt O Björklund left his native Sweden bound for India to seek his hippie dreams in 1968, but ended up in a Turkish prison for possession of a small amount of hashish. A portion of this story was creatively represented in the movie Midnight Express.

During his imprisonment Bengt wrote his first poems and songs and also began painting. After his release he resettled in his homeland and began to paint and write, play music and perform his work.

"Time is a lake fed by the moon."

Well within the tradition and literary scope of experimental language employed by beat poets, Bengt uses what might be described as an avant-garde non-fiction, stream of consciousness in this long poem series.

"I see that you are another me I
that holy is such a very short time"

Employing a combination of narrative, culturo-generational commentary, and shifts in source perspective, he has created a wide field in which to better paint the scope of impression, sentiment, lament, wisdom, woe and philosophy gleaned from the span of a lifetime.

"Hear! War is not a language"

Instead of the poems in I standing as solitary trees in a field, they more resemble a grove of aspen trees having a complex underground root source from which each individual poem sprouts and grows. What at first seems reminescent of Joyce's Ulysses becomes, through engaged reading, something more closely resembling Gilles Deleuze's concept of a Plane of Immanence.

"There is a final blessing
it is so human."

— *David Anthony Martin*
author of Span, Deepening the Map, Bijoux and Founding
Editor of Middle Creek Publishing

I

BENGT O BJÖRKLUND

I

© **2018, Bengt O. Björklund**

No part of this book may be reproduced by any means known at this time or derived henceforth without written permission of the publisher or author. The exception would be in the case of brief quotations embodied in the critical articles or reviews and pages where permission is specifically granted by the publisher or author.

Books may be purchased in quantity and/or special sales by contacting the publisher. All inquiries related to such matters should be addressed to:

Middle Creek Publishing & Audio
9027 Cascade Avenue
Beulah, CO 81023
editor@middlecreekpublishing.com
(719) 369-9050

Author Image: Bengt. O Björklund
Cover Design: David A. Martin,
Middle Creek Publishing
Printed in the United States

First Edition, 2018

ISBN: 978-0-9989322-5-5

I

BENGT O BJÖRKLUND

Middle Creek Publishing & Audio
Beulah, CO •USA

↑

Dedication

So many people have been crucial to my continuous effort to write the perfect poem, but still I have not succeeded. I hope I never will.

But without my mother I would not be, without my sisters I'd have no early bearing. All my previous wives have acknowledged the fact that I am a poet, but Gertrude, the last one, actually reads my poems!

Thank you David Martin for actually seeing something in these poems that touched you and made you go through this long processes of editing three years of unpublished poetry.

Thank you Dominic Williams, the first publisher to introduce me to the English spoken world. Dylan Thomas brought us together.

And thank you Billy Hayes for writing a few words of introduction. All the best!

Thank you P2 Världen for all the music

It is in the green
of the ancient night
summer flustered
with a spinning destiny
I hear trees talk

old trees young trees shrubs
humming like dynamos
with the I lost in breath
and a watery voice
beneath the calling
of so much more

a viscous night
runny with a cockled sea
beneath a bright spring moon
pulling smooth water at will
in eyes believing

man made waves roll
fish bite in the dark
mariner seaweed
teem with brutal extinction
the phantom is a feeding chain

the night is an old clock
a watery pendulum ticking
swinging spidery legs
over a wet weight of sand
where I will not sleep

~

one man I walking
across still I rolling
country hills
once perceived
in a Turkish dream
reaping the end

a dream birthed me
in eastern jail austerity
I was so much younger
than I really care to
consider any more

speeding outside the window
one is a tide in a new spring
rolling over dragon-swept hills
the other is newly shorn sheep
looking small and forlorn

this is the quick sea salt walk
one might pick up and see
in time for green time tickling
commons in confusion
lost in battle lost for ever

~

coming alive in seconds
is like dancing
dancing to the sound
of the one time falling
a breath of music
throbbing in shabby dwellings
down steep sides of hills
where heart-life is but
a small puny bargain

I called you one night
on the magic telephone
but there was no bleak heaven
darkened by the dark splendor
to accept the charges
leaking like an old faucet
forestall impeding silence

I saw you leaving it all
to invisible hands
scurrying for increased profit
in sands of no more
I saw you there and stayed
while carving I walked with you
in a different part of town

~

I am the impeding
of what must come around
the inevitability of things
we call home

hush - look at me -
I am still here
bleeding across
your eyes on the floor

there is no merry pardon
no dark mistress
undressing for your eyes
only this futility

I am the one more day
the one more breath
the one more at all
of all that is all no more

~

rapturous I in tall times
of bleeding bleeding
in shiny halls of no more
I in the suddenness

of nights in late spring running
with more hues of green
than any eye possibly
can register in rain
chosen for its austerity
among the dying

I was more than a failure
I was a certain ticking
of an inevitability
unplugging all hope
pulling the cap
grinning with skulls
in a frozen smile
I was more than not
more than getting hold
of the last word

~

I saw you this morning
naked just before I woke up
seeking wild sex ecstasy
with fingers of an old world
but when you called me
I woke up and a grey sky
walking over cold water still
put me under the cherry tree
I saw ducks feeding in mirrors

reflecting a slow green burst
of birches' wanting to survive
scolded by bleak May-winds

libation is still important
rituals of contact war
shedding soft soldiers into
the final fire of star cruelty

armies have that effect
on poets and painters
on tinkers and squatters
on all opposed to odium

see me here see me not here
it is all a matter of
who still have a say so
and who has not

there are a billion pauses
between the two sides
where one actually
can write something

I kept taking my clothes off
in front of windows
before my own lurid mirror
but I did not die there

~

with too many why-not's
to fill the coming of the rest of it
it makes no difference if the sky
folds into neat piles of transparency
or if the what comes after
holds whatever key to unlock
entrances in blinding flames
sealed and forgotten in tomorrow's gold
and like I told you so

between you and me
you can see the short of it
the handle on the bar
the sweet told you so
when night finds you all dark
in a hot pile of ashes
scorched with old matches
misfired worn out
frail and ridiculed for being undone
in an advanced farewell

this bloody day farewell
that no cure can heal from pain
keeps anger on the run
and little men feeding
their imaginary ego shadows
this rotten darkness served

is solitary man's burning farewell
sinister men congregate
grass wilt and die

~

solemnity is a charred ego past
fuming like a serpent settlement
in the annals of the sacred
I hear tonalities of the old ways
soaring through the greens
while on a walk in slow spring

nailed burned and shot
is all frosty darkness
any history can muster

the harbingers of adoration
still fuzz in winds and streams
where heart is one

suddenness is more of the same
grey afternoon slurs
rolls into a big toothless thunder

darkness meets darkness
sinister ominous and dead
adored you sit at the table

there are no buoyant truths
beneath the cherry tree
nor in the coming of rain

muster your skills and dance
there are mires on the move
staleness is in your way

the children could not see
the dead could not talk
the war raged until morning

~

it was the first heron birth ascending
- rolling on high shores
in a prison cell of old Istanbul
with a cockled heart elevated high
in a musky smell of a child's wet sand -
that started the fire
a breath a way out an epiphany
he talked to me in long dreams
before daybreak spelled my name
and day soaked long diction in vivacity
before he landed on my Spartan bed
feeding my eyes with Wales

~

symbiotic is my love
clinging to the last rays of stars
in brevity shining
in bright halls of more spring
charged with a swirling force
constantly calling me by name

this love loaded and ready to go
is not a plea nor a whisper
it is the short term embodiment
of everything I hold close
when my illusionary heart breaks

I am a cry for total mercy
a voice with the poor
to stand up with a joyous roar
a demand for peace
and tales and good will

pure intent and walking merrily
on wishful wires

this love I is lethal I say
this love you this love you see
a tree and a plant the sky
above the roaring sea
madness beyond madness
a quick flicker on water's edge

a blink in the every one eye
where I reside and die

~

it is not in the I
you chose to say good bye
it is not in a time
given by the heaving sea
seamen search and travel
and in the end
there can only be one
verified Indian at the table

I see dogs being closer
to the love I know
than me and you traveling
for the sake of it

night is a sweet mistress
and I am unfaithful
burrowing and clinging
to a pale rabbit moon

see me not then
in the little house
clinging to the old cliff
shifting paper shifting

sea salt singing
in the western wind
wayward is the name of he
that I walk to the end

ceremonial I walk the day
where continuity breaks
all conventions
to the sound of more waves

~

circles of wishful fire
are no longer merry or bright
around that of worth

streams of I is I
shift gear
while there is still time

see me not then
in gloss or fountains
where I am not

see me and see not
I will be here
as long as it takes

~

so many slow seas
dead people on the increase
flowers and succulent trees
blue babies sleeping among peas
aquariums and a golden fleece
stipulations and pure lunacies
it is all a question of serenities
the way you use your panic keys
in a room full of winds with no pities

roads unfold and roll with day
never questioned nor, I'd say,
fed with the poison you must pay
in time for yet another play
on roads that crawl with grey
and dreary ongoing, if you may,
telling tales of time to spare
of crimes pardoned in the where
all is a sanctioned shattered share

~

I am slow fire burning
at the end of another day
a living talisman

a charm you may touch
and hope for the rest

there are men in trees
riding the wind
with resin and limbs
joined by the hip in observation
from the I and the other I

there is solemnity
in speedometers that
no longer are in use
perception is all
one man can be

there is a breath
breathing
a focus yearning
for that which soon
will be gone

~

be gone solitude in sallow moon
pulling rainy legs in slow tide rolling
with spiders of a different day plotting
in a sorely prolonged aftermath

I am the not I folding evenings
into mediocrities and swollen egos
I am the sail into your own story
the fallout of graced focus

fooled loved and so utterly dead
a beauty in a last standing
turning wide open to a tiny praise
short time stamina thrives on

tell me woman tell me
this lyrical dying
this side of being here
does it move you

she looked at me
in desperation
sighing heaving moving
with the otherness
rhythm can meet at times

slow me take me
for the short term I am
a want to have
breathing pulsating

the universe is no comfort
the no beginning no end
the multi billion
vast stellar backdrop

I am the he in last night falling
conceptually twisted
wrought in cellular stuff
breathing sighing slowly dying

~

there is a certain slow touch
to evening folding
with all one can wish for

suggestive and swift
there are keyboard players
attacking the radio
it's all about the basics
magpies bagpipes
welsh herons at the end

a brevity longer than
any shadow falling
this side of sizzling equator

it's all about the amount
the shift the drive the go
the all that will pass

one is a cool break
where lunar tides break
over this side of matter

saturated dipped and worn
there is a finality
in the everything that lives

I remember you and you
glittering like sunny waves
in a gushing memory
I remember and yet I die
with every breath I take
with every move I make

see the I the you
the nothing more in shadows
heading for dusk

no more I no more you
in all that matters
no more more no
see the me in great love
with this all I must embrace
magic on tour on line
where I in mad bliss dance
while still urgently inhaling
promises of I know
to be taken seriously

in a summer rolling
with chlorophyll and yearning
there can be no other

a love of all
that moves on Earth
nodding to a slow future

yesterday's I do not know
lurks in the no-answers
I cannot see
laughing at the brain police
riding inflicted horses
taking you straight to here

where there are more
and so many more yet

~

thick and layered with green
I breathe in sighs and leave
with the heavy longing of grass

tell me suitor and wild ender of days
where can one find relief
from pondering upon the door

night fell like a thin tailed comet
a streaking afternoon attention
with a thousand good byes

there was wild music seeping
through the ins and outs
there was an impossible longing

~

solitude embracing sad suns
riding at the edge of understanding
it is the way the world breaks
on a Tuesday full of doubt
willfully she leaves green footprints
across the what the children will find
when universal is yet a step closer
to the constant middle of it all

sleep me drool me cascade me
in the here of life's short dominion
where air is constantly produced
at the cost of breaking secretes

there are folks that roll in silent ragas
that elope in fugues of old
that see no more than monk choirs
breaking at the crack of dawn

~

in the glory of death says so
I find fuel and rebels to go
I find it all funny and turning
like candles and cars burning

I see midnights I see the end
I see streetcars roll and bend
I see trees in a living folly here
where truly nothing avails a tear

seek me here seek me not
this voice still living still hot
it is a matter of tabled time
of being where no bells can chime

drive my wedge fill my shoe
soon there will be no more no go
sailors fall into the roaring sea
the I is no longer a me

~

steal me feed me die me
in days of slow comprehension
drive me up the dark country
seep me through a wiry extension

drilled in back water shoals
I often fish while sleeping

in trees by summer schools
with the sun silently creeping

dovetailed and winged today
I slept you across the scary hall
where man made machines pray
for the almost dead to make a last call

find me not in disarray
where I river blind survive
where the silent I can play
find me not so unkind and alive

time for another day done
with I somewhere in motivation
in an oxygen relief gone
deep into its own ramification

~

summer is best ingested
with swallows in flight
armories make you congested
with fury in a fiery might

I see you with a shovel walking
never reversing while talking

with flowers sunrays and a beer
I move festive trees in a song
where badgers roam and deer
really – what could go wrong

I see you moving stones and time
in a looming booming with lime

when the sun in us is heavily set
behind the earth that moves today
there can be no summary regret
no antimatter coming out to play

I loved you rolling in the sun
heavily smiled with I on the run

ditched in a bright light calling
I see no heated danger yet
in day's burning breath falling
extinction is just a bet

hold a hot eye to the day I make
with so much hot ash to rake

~

wish upon a bright sky folds tonight
with solitude and a cohort so in love

that matter bends perceptions of light
into no more aiming for the I above

all lost I's find ways of saying so
breaking on shores of short times done
grabbing the long of it by the silent row
dying for brimstone dimes of the old sun

tell me brotherly one in silence fold
what is the meaning of nothing in all
when borders burn and legacies fold
when the one and only is a long distance call

serenity is a luxury paid for in lost times
and guiles of cruel savors in tents is the price
wanton seals on every other day I in crime
sell deeds by the rolling of a fickle dice

reset you look for old bathroom doors
where the house tilts to the west
where I and I make love and settle scores
before waking hours are put to rest

~

ceremonies of total madness
bleat under dead moon rising
in just another show to tell
of what really goes on

holy men without money
pray for more sex with minors
holy mothers of the cloth
ship out to dictate the difference
between what embarrasses

a pious flag
from a loaf of bread

I run red with blood
children women and men
not in favor of war

there is no alliance
with the meek
no excuse for losing
interest in I

there is a no more hello
in the all of everything
in the finality that finally
comes into a sedimentary play

hello hi
I am here
do you remember me
do you see me

find other I:s
where all you
reconvene

and finally
has a final say

~

seriously tilting at day's
shifting into summer pajamas
winds hold back
oceans of continental air
roll in from the north
with soft sighs rising
of lovers you once held

the drummer is another one
moving along
finding breath and motion
joined by expression
lifting the magic of rhythm
to a soft tissue paper sky
a short while-burning time

a rose is planted today
the sky is in so many shades
of blue and the grey of me
it makes no difference

if you long for it all
if you live it all
it can be only one

~

serenity leads to treason
dark betrayal
subversion and mockery
you will call reality
a killing by the beast
the worst of it
falling like a nail's rain
spikes that bleed
till the end of what you need

usurpers of rotten time
wind their clocks
in a different fashion
than walkers on high wire
there is no stopping
bash beheading traumas
rolling like chemical blood
around the dying of the feet

herbs in validation
burn where the heart is
liquid gold runs with thirst
one is all one needs

to fulfill the dream of he
that sweeps all entirety
with slow consequence

serenity is just another reason
why violent men run
with dark guns
why slow reason retreats
why camera men
look for houses
in different parts of town
why the sinister
always have an advantage

~

a brain is a dynamo
constantly discovering
its own short fused hums
of electric supply
in the forever looking
for a meaning in a cortex
of human perspective
making no more sense
than a vineyard on the run
from the end closing in
to where air that is
only is what is
a breeze a sail a wave

breaking at the edge
of old memory

~

see me Seamus how I say
with the all I was given
see me here see me play
see how far I have driven

it was day going into night
summer fields blooming
what I saw shone so bright
like a pigeon I was homing

love the reason you can hear
rolling like a dicey tide
there are no reason left to fear
alone on your rickety ride

seamstress' and seamen
play in the reed
without now without then
this is the fruit of your seed

Seamus I mean to say
there is not even a here

in what I or you may
or not find in feral fear

~

I see the will not cry
the will not sleep in derma extinction

with hearts exploding over meat markets
slithering in confusion I

rosaries burn for interpretation
old symbols thrust against the other
just for the sake of being safe
there is a no more in all acuity

there are days for anything to be
for endings and let go to wander
there is so much before nothing
I is the one to be in still here

~

repeatedly in summer flustered with I
one flies with distant promises of still here
while I in the I look at a very lush sky
there's a billing of there is nothing more to fear

thunder rolls with eggs and squirrels
in the early morning of another I can see
there's no peace in the I clock tale bells
or in the dying of the blue night sea

one walked immersed in water words
birds and the falling of a cockled sea

another was lost in a sea of I weed herds
tolling like I innermost in a final me

~

I is the conscious entity of any man
at the crossroad of nothing at all
on shores and streets

I am the causality I am
to any observational say so
of the tangible

there is undelivered time
unborn emptiness where I
no longer cry for more

I in the eye of any man
is soon history
tales and mystery
I am the I crying in the eye of I

I am the why and the I am no more
I am the short of any I here

~

I sing the song of I
rolling like dark thunder
amongst the new-born
breaking like murky ice
when war is receding
from the front page
to a mere mention on page 7

I sing the song of I
in the ruins of so many cities
where flesh is just greed
and solemnity
only a bargain to go
before suicide bombers
wreck what is left

I sing the song of I
amongst the holy men
lusting for boys
amongst the speakers of hate
the mongers of stolen time
the slashers and the cut throats
I sing the song of I
in the rotting leftovers

in dumpsters
amongst hookers and low life
waiting for one more fix

amongst the break ups
and the sore to go

I sing the song of I
every day I see you smile
every day I see I
in opposition and why
my eyes have no blinds
no power to bend light

I sing the song of I
as long as I can
to the oncoming traffic
the debris and flotsam
the swirling vortex
of dark water

I sing the song of I
to the dying of the day
to the memory of another I
long dead
there's another I that I can see
in all that is left
I sing the song of I
I am the song of I

~

so I belong to the ancient ones
roaming with shifting days
in a continuous relay singing
from one man to the next

this I chained to the sea
is all we have in any weather
a call across the ticking brevity
of a last breath wheezing

I need you more when the sea
like a dark mother calls my name
and the wind prepares the children
for a memory of another I

~

I see you in I umbra of shadows
with scrapings of hurrying crabs in tides
baring all in between in a singular why

the shaman lived in a rundown penthouse
high above the shameless São Paulo bustle
with his freebase and binoculars

the last prism is a broken solitude
a paradigm a gasp for contact
where bets no longer is a young body

create me dive me sleep me
there are no concessions left
to run tomorrow's carry on

but there are meetings above ground
in abandoned non light houses
with brooms on the run from Bogota

sleep me in domes of darkness
drive me down a last good night
soon all will be a deep breath

I am the roller-coaster I in you
finding looking long for mires
to set sail at bit over the moon

~

there is panic in the I
slowly eaten by sharp hours
with knifes of unbridled indifference
I saw you leave I behind
in a motion of no more hands
peeled like an onion in the sky
the wind died from one day

to a very silent next of kin
fading in a far away so and so

fear is the mother of silence
indifference is the fall between
all yesterday's thunder

the slate I am will be wiped
in one single brutal sweep
just before I no longer is a name

there is cold beer for the giants
long green goodbyes
by old streets of yesterday gone

~

nothing can outlast the coming
of days like thunder rolling
arid times like these that echoes
too many summers on the line

a cold beer down by the pond
a soft breeze in the late afternoon
I can still hear the dead sigh
in the still silence of grass

I rest my weary case on the sill
high on seeing the day at will

and yet and still
walk the memory plank I will

~

lost in the floriferous I
the green I
the green summer of I

there's an impossible dream here
in bed with old age bending I
holding on to a child's promises

there is no other I in this room
no other no more no less
and still the green I is the summer

I am the blue sky electrified
when I look at you sky and heart
I am the I of these words

I am all you can see I
the only solid wind moving
I can be in days of me I

~

human burdens are all we have
ungodly faces we cannot escape
moving like singed rats running
across burning cardboard steamships

can I have this dance please
the summer is blocking the view
all my dark intentions need
to move mountains and roads

there is an ire I do not aspire
in the motion of the collective I
the I fed up with reeking wastewater
bubbling out of control

I've seen the mythological tail
the horns the hooves
the malicious eye glaring
at my lost glen serenity

the last photo was taken
just before empty sky paled
there were no reason
to give a rat's ass or I

still one must love
the magic of being inertly alive
blowing steam into double horns
from here to the arid end I

~

soar you lethal bird bold with future
the ocean is a mere foothold
where I in an unrequited prayer look
for answers in tides breaking
no winged priest or drunk master
of yesterday's ceremonies gone
can walk sandy traps of yesterday
without leaving hieroglyphics behind

you glare at poor man's meal
you want him water locked dead
you want him in sand erased
gone from superior views you

this world is an infestation
a cancer ridden hippodrome running
love is poor man's saddle
a sighing wind I will be the end

~

I am the antithesis of the I
all in doubt
the reason it all comes down to
tumbling like weed
on a freeway to nowhere

I am the very cause
the fallout the rain the soot
cotton mills of old
succumbing to the history
where palaces are made of tarot cards
turtle whisper and sticks

the very end of I as you know I
in days where I am I
still carries meaning all the way
to the shores of no memory

I one might add I and more
the struggle for meaning
keep on winding sudden dips
into stray stars and beaches
where a stitch is no hex just fun
where I is a late promise
fading into the rolling

of more sugar and lame talk
crutches and ducking

I am a golden melon stay
a me trickle of lethal pay
a clock going the other way
turning day into final day

I am lost epiphany in a dragon smoke
a weird creature climbing the soil of memory

on ladders planted on the smelly mire floor
just for the sake of breathing bleeding
in a laid back song of dark matter

"sedimentary" a voice whispered to me
"sedimentary and basically
a grave grief on the run"
I saw no reason to enter a plea
I had no time to make a call

there is a certain strangeness
going around like a cold
or a poriferous flu
a matter of seeing or interpreting
making dullness a fulfillment
of a dying child in you

I will not be there
when rodents rule the world
I am the I and the you I
we did what we could

~

juiced by pale moon September
I cautiously venture into veins
where I walking still can remember
all my losses and all my gains

roaring sea of don't mention it
rolls on a temporary shore
where brief I and others still sit
dreaming of days with much more

~

there is no I in the why of today calling
it is not in the I of yesterday's groveling
before the emptiness of a flayed sky I sing
there are consequences in the I falling

leveled erased washed into the sea
I can no longer see when I cease to be
the sun is an I in a universe in me
there are so many reasons not to be

~

dying is easy when tides turn
and see-through jellyfish
look at you in dismay

bow upon stringed bow
line the ancient battlement
beneath an anesthetized moon

it is the night of call me no more
of rifts hanging like ripe oranges
just before dark is not a name

~

so you think you can think
one man against the onslaught
of history and hate's change

you think you matter
when the pale one stab you
for being the only one
not carrying arms

I see your burning grass
the soft ones dying in slow water
too much sorrow in one's day
will always be wrong

I dare you to see the why
these words can be all
a left behind time grinning
will find relevant

laugh with me see the curve
understanding can make
unfolding Is into I in you
drinking fascination liked rain

see the me in the I of you
in the raw window-shopping
where the I meandering
is only I going home

~

everyday darkness rolls out of darkness
spewing itself into a world
where the self-esteem of the righteous
laugh at the me and the softly spoken
because we burn with attention
with hungry fire fear to die

darkness will fall asleep like a drunkard
smoldering in dreams of silent tyranny
the sensation of winds will swirl
faster and more to the faces laughing
darkness will take what it wants
walking all over comprehension

salutations to sallow moon ticking
for brave men walking alone
breaking like waves of no tomorrow
there are other men at work
vessels leave vessels return
songs roll like sharp salt in the wind

serpent-like coiled fetus guarding
the fragility of I borne into I see
wherever I find a reason to do so
gamble on number seven

the day is a thing of the eye
there are no wake up calls

~

I walk the nudity of broken chains
wallowing in tides rolling with the weed
to put a smile back on the old man

once in such a time on its own
I walked the cruelty of the commodity
with today breaking mirrors breathing

I see the hear me and the see you calling
in wells of not so good bellowing in smoke
so what's in it for me on a windy day

when I see you and you in the I see
I am more than water in a deed gone air
time is a pillow by a child's fountain

~

cryptic in cold winds
I foil the priestly heron
guarding the heritage sermon
pressing wet sand
beneath an old boathouse

the cove in its bending grace
replenished and empty again
holds the eye captive to the I
to the damp smell of hinges
flapping with bird wings

eyes retreat in sand and surf
roll into findings of poor shields
where wild lilies will not hear
the weary sea song calling
to the one water orchestra

~

drugged out patients run
in billion dollar spams
fools you with outrageous promises
of more time and money to go
just to keep you in line

hollering owls at your mercy
roll the dice at midnight eye fleeing
seemingly at ease melting

beneath the onslaught of hate
when there is no need

the gluttonous grieve in silence
the solemn lose their echo
there are billions more
looking for a different ride
the number of stations is finite

~

I in the wind I turned
to whirling birds in showers
of a new end returning

I often find myself in an element
beating birds on the windowsill
lighthouse erected into night

~

"salutations" wild man shouted
loading his gun with transparent water
"there is only one way to go"
he looked like he wanted to laugh

there are dead people rolling in the tide
smirks never meant for the public

I see soldiers fulfill the dreams of the dead
rolling their dark intents across the sand

"salutations" he walked faster now
rocking with the tide rolling on his back
"there is no time" he paused "there is a need"
he was not running for the last train

~

she walked dark cloud
talked tilting house
spewing ash and adrenalin on all
with a rash to a different tune

she spoke backwards
and ordered in dire need
a deed done is but another dare
a flare to singe with

empty buildings on the run
anger brewing like salt in the sun
a fault is carelessly carved
from a loaf of stale bread

there is no direction here
just the fall of endless waves
on sand groveling for more
a dark tale indeed

~

sailed to the windy void
where suddenness
is a chain in command
I see your grief
beaten by the centennial
I see weary ones
hammering at icy sky

barren in the end year salt
casks roll in dark refusal
with eavesdropping stethoscopes
small pirates have stolen
in dark cloud incidents
fine headed nails
will drive you for a small fee

~

driven with bells sounding loud
I see no other I as road dips into red
recollections on fire flaming high
with words at the end of empty barrels

scrolled like the ancients poor memory
I steam refusals like a powdered gun man

caught in the sullen room of claws and theft
with only a towel and a death certificate

young men die young and coarse religion
crawls chafed and burning hard
more men are rolling in the waves tonight
there is a subtle reference to decomposition

it's the juggling season you see
homage is just another page
singing red and wet and final
we are dogs hovering on line

~

death is not a sterile shine
on a kitchen sink in oblivion
a blast a dent a surprise
jumping from darkness
into a different darkness

there's a tide in a dream
rolling ever faster
over silent sand submission
there is a light switch
no one can find

there is panic in all words
copper pipes are breaking

to the sound of doctors running
weird tones collapse
on fake Persian carpets

brutality is poor man's frustration
see his lizard bleeding
the dead in ire feeding
the psycho goat needs a speaker
brutality needs surgery

~

these are gurney-rolling kind of days
dark druid bottles of dark ale
are tempted by wild innards of I
in a slaughter kind of a fashion

dreamt scourged remnants bones
limbs by number I
there is so much for the hell of it
for the I cannot tell the difference
between a gun or a loaded carrot

stones need no stereo effect
there are gaps in the retelling
sleep is not an option
gentle does not come into it

~

stretched like a dying moon
across day melt down horizon

I see no reason not to sneer at
small people see no navel

wrapped like a ghetto street
'round the aspiration and the rest
I lose my breath beat no more
strong is my resolve frail

sing family I sing history and it
the fall you expected and paid for
the shortness of moving closer
a kind of diving a trust a bated breath

~

shallow nights I will not go
spidery legs will beg the other way

there are houses with thin pages
there is no food on the table

cold wet so soaked to the tent
cardboard wilting in November

fetid Europe salutes in fancy knickers
at brown uniformed funerals

swollen with vengeance and the dead
all protest will eventually decompose

leaves blanket circular autumn
seasonal exhalation is tall

there will be no accountability
but a pleading blink of a small child

there will be a no more the same
with a no content in hungry stalkers

I walk with pale understanding
to the end of each day uncertain

~

tolling no more on dark nights
seriously bound and gagged I wound
is a knot to be swallowed with rain

there is an epitaph no diploma
weariness will corrode in time told
there will be many ceremonies

take good care of the children
burning in the war of the anonymous
their hands will not do what we predict

no more zebra crossing winking lost
stale memory warfare is dust is not
like I you in a universal flash gone

There is a murderous theocracy
in a pompous petri dish
vengeance in a gutter calling
pity pity soldier boy dying
the crowd that stood and stared
it will pass with no pain

no hills no sea just a studio
ale on the rocks of the imaginary
a blanket a veil a whisper not

~

merchant of dark time infusion
matters more to infants crying
than death in an empty testament
no collusion of the cloth will shine
there will be no literal say so
transparent in no shame

there are billions and billions
and there is nothing
tonight I will see you here

tomorrow yes here
I miss you
this is what I am

~

spoiled by religion and war
little man clings to the book
straps his cold coin sorrow
to the chest of a last day

he who will not wallow in bitter I
abolishing all claims and holds
he will be the I to bleed no more
in better days perhaps or not

dark fruit rotting in sinister night
murderous madness longing for water
there are no safe haven eyes
there is only I you see a fire fly

smoldering sobbing with words
there can be no two eyes holding

only the throbbing masses of no I
running with greed malice and reptile

belonging is not a psychotic girl
shooting amphetamine to pass the blame
the first frost flew in silence
there were no chores no hands

~

solemnity rises into the coming
of fire in a different hour
rolls like soft glass
in honor of the day's ending

there are more than one
to each slot on the Ouija board
tilting with secrets and silence
but the dead will not speak

~

a wave a death wish
rolls in cold November
no one sees the naked sailor
or the flag-semaphore
signaling at the end

the need to crystallize
comes with the season
waving its magic
where still water shifts
when no one is watching

see me in the good night
still with a smile
for the beating heart

see me here the I herald
of younger days to come

~

semiotic and silenced by madness
you interpret I in a different way
your own quiet storm unfolds
as you listen to talk of weather and ice
sleep is not in your best interest
you dance to music only you can hear

I saw you in a dog swollen cold November
a bitch bloated in the ongoing of life
waiting for a final curtain call
I called out for a vet any vet
you roamed ahead a broke the wind
with eyes runny with nothing

steepled and towered above frosty roofs
I remember a Russian that never lost
his early years to beast or bottle
representing impossible hope I
with few days of reckon and embrace
listening to the ice dressing the water

~

staring in the face of nothing more
I see you and the children dancing
the northern dance of winter's light

so much afterthought in the old furnace
so many pellets of good intentions
burning into aftermath's longing

still walked and withered
to the brittle bone of old age
I refuse the math the numbers

sanctioned by the random
paid for by the resistance
I have no other excuse

~

there are elements in the draw
soft skin that slide sideways
through the fallout centers

time is a bottle of spiced honey
the rattling of winter's grass
a lethal sigh in the dark of I

rewarding ceremonials are in repeat
cautiousness is an acquired taste
a quiver a yearning a desperation

winter sand ticking rivers and ice
baleful intent rotting in plain view
there is a genetic consequence

I am the I that is you in the I
it is getting dark
there must be more to fire

~

leveled in days on the run
subdued and abandoned
like a basket baby
on the steps of an empty church
where the wind dies
a love strong like the sea
rolled its winter dice silence

above translucent grass
there is a magpie
in the tree outside my window

sky grey tolls and calls
birds and graves will gather
at the end of the road
there are rumors
of a hostile take over

there are times when motion
is just a notion of breathing
in days when all is still birth
the sky's a ruptured egg
I death has a different smell

~

so much weariness walking wild
books without covers are flogged
in tales to dark to tell

he is the dead keeper walking
summoning the one thing
all weather can agree upon

steeped in thick silenced tea
solitary and bereaved he sinks
with no taste of sugar

67

"dare me not" he whispers
far into the coming night
"dare me not I am he"

~

so many rivers to hail
days with bassoon and harp
fade in the afterbirth

ceremonies of bewilderment
tokens of ephemeral now in awe
I am not a winter forest

the dance of the freezing
sings in a winter pond
shrouded in shadows

given to walks between the I
and the last of it all
beauty lives to the a different sound

"the end game" she whispered
"there is still more to do
in the arms of death"

~

seashore ramblings
under
dark waves
with no further
ado
a sigh
a breath

there are bills
body credits
sales
children burning
like silk
paper
for a cause

we are bottles
looking for
eternal spirits
finding clocks
war
ticking sand
and a sadness to go

~

transforming cellular yearnings
of totaling all days

I find calls to the winter moon
a different kind of lunacy

there are cats in the machinery
wolves in the downfall

serpents in the carpentry
of old history

the blinking of a culture
sedimentary believes
are days that belong
the eyes of the universe

~

who is he that I am not
rolling dark thunder
just for the sake of bright lights
and a dance to go

ceremonial occurrences of today
do not proclaim solid kingdoms
in anyone's slow perception
it is all a matter of reliance

conviction is a lack of wisdom
sometimes though

there is no point in getting mad
for the sake of an old book

there is a dead silence creeping
through the aftermath of border control
it's less than a road's end challenge
more like so much fatigue

~

momentary blows to the heart
bring back another baleful tale

from the backburner
and still

soft tissue cannot stipulate
the existence of a perpetual anything

waves on eternal shores without mercy
is not a continuity of singularity
staggering between despair and no hope
and yet this mad love
this tenderness
that haunts the empty heart I

~

incendiary devices ignite day's duality
one for the road and one for the emptiness
there are samples of true illusion
by the daily gate of I told you so and more

wish there were something more to airwaves
moving short feet seaweed hair forest lost
just one more silly hand out of potion
in hallways with caryatids in mourning

must love this Russian composition
that rolls thunderous dark into green spliffs
ignited and believed in by small crowds
in an attempt at forgetfulness

last man woe briefly stands
in wait of the clipping of the ticket
there is no winner no count down
no trace no pass go in emptiness

~

thus the grand was left
to its own unmaking
where a wishing tree was planted
he plunged deep into the void and died
there where no remedies
just a pain called the short of it

the night was a rolling dark sea
over all our short endings
I am a gardener

dribble the earth and fly
birds are ticking in bushes
do not speak of hands

~

I give you the endless
a fruit in need of consumption

two is always a need of one
in time for curtain fall

there is grave misconception
amongst the wise and good

telltale is a balloon released
a monitor on the run

it is only I on the run
a here for the living
a bracket with my name
an immediacy no beyond

~

winter night ruminates
polished and ready
over quick done in darkness

slow hands run
through gloomy sand's hair
with salty dog in charge

it is a night of reckoning
vile wings of yesterday
beat at yesterday's brow

at one point there was a one
solidifying all hours
now all days are behind the trees

~

it's in the expectancy I fall
waiting for the bus
a cold winter day standing
by the end of tomorrow
solidified by subzero winds
one invents a new mean
to keep all soldiers in line
believing in the glory of dying

this is yesterday's tomorrow
no better no worse

colliding with the human heart
perceived by all to be dead

~

so the heart is buried
in a place timed by the turning
and soft tissue heaving

vigorously diving
the one retrieves salt and beads
from the brow of the poor

I see lightning
ripping distant hearts
into watery shreds

solemnity is a car
running slowly off track
in its own wake

~

do not whisper I waves
in tidal approach

do not sleep in dry ink beds
do not enter into words like after

I sing these lines at will
drawl and drag syntax
with an unruly forest making
I in time to be here

I sing death by day doing
linger in the fabric of I lore
dessert is a lost promise
of still sand I that I am

walkover ocean seeded you
the instant you eyed it
daring the rest not to end up
in sea-wind ruptured darkness

there is a no more in the making
running with fired feet

from end game gambled
to a constantly no more

~

driven by I here days
with a taste for fake eternity
I itch for my skin
to fold measures into time

I the sun is a dragon mother
smoldering with immanence

it's all for the short of it
and the must let go

"vernal promises hurt"
she whispered from treetops
withdrawn in late winter snow
loaded with latency

~

a spidery walk on windows
a chimney in bleak dismay
wharfs bleeding for years
in tides that will never come

bitten by the weather
rolled like a windy dice

night is a sallow mistress
a full moon with a roof

driven I say driven
to the point of no point

one must concede and fold
with no more why in the wind

~

the smell of soft ice melting
at this time of year
is a solace to the count of ten

bones and tissue sing I am
the old dog moves the ash
in the old wood urn

there were others born
into my lost custody
I mislaid them

~

time is a lake fed by the moon
solitude runs by itself for days
birds are lost in the machinery
where feathers grease progress

there is a mountain by that lake
a waterfall that roars to heaven

with rainbows flickering
and deities laughing at beggars cry

semiotic madness drives the poet
with metaphors ending beauty with death
with visions that flicker at the rim
of every day solitude ending

serendipity is a matter of why
one man meets his destiny
with eyes held high above the wind
and others just fold and fade

~

sand the bloody weight of sand
snaky oil coils of folded time
the all of it calling on folly
for new appearances in wet halls
where bright herons feed
it is I but I blowing riddled smoke
over the infamous the sadly affected
the sorrow of I you in this world
of badly beaten shadows
where nothing is not possible

~

down the foothills of memory
sprawled I like a starfish
dying in the morning sun

I can but allow you
the satisfaction
of my own beloved doubt

tenderness does not fly
in villages where bombs burst
in the light of a billions suns

I am not the benefactor of alarms
nor the two timed suicide driver
ringing once for time to end

salutations are in order
when the I seeing
is a dark blue sky on the run

~

so many different voices
the sky is an eggshell

a pale azure revolving
over these voices

I flicker and die at will
with sun and birds
testifying to the living
with thin voices

in the sky shaped skull
I like in a reed basket

make my own words
and these voices

brick and mortar are we
sludge dreaming in storm drains
this day is nothing more than
a thin voice on the run

in all the I and their words
a fire is burning with elements
and all the I
succumbs to these voices

~

visualized at the beginning
merely as a grand piano
with keys running for cover
I see small men fleeing
manmade evil cringing cowed
saluting even lesser men
drinking from toilets of tomorrow
residing in ballots and arms
driving insanity like noisy trams
before the Dam square drug squad
intimidated by Japanese tourists
and baby dove commuters

stretched like a rubber arm
around the epicenter of collision
I find you like I and no more
tap dancing on windowsills falling
certain of a final failure
where goalkeepers feed their runs
winds never roll
where there is no consolation
no bastard redemption
no awards for the meek or the poor
where night is no alternative
I find darkness to be any man's foreplay

~

it's in the dread of nothingness
empty words wander incessantly
daring good men to do battle
where a vicious void bleed
for the sake of a name or a field

I will not see to the I summoned
cared for by specters of dark shine
no sermon intends delivery of wit
in time for seasonal changes to heave
with eyes crossed by religion and sneers

strapped by the holier than I
night wrapped its hurting content

'round imagine an old birch
pleased with roots to branch
attentive to the moons silence

~

the moon is a serum
injected by the foaming sea
where I you see hooked
finds the light you

served skinless and so dead
the one still mumbles
in hallways and tumbles
to the sound of keys

versified mothers and more
dance to the I singing
above the silenced battlefields
where I is of no consequence

told by the shanty many
there is a hum growing in the sky
a kind of breathing in space
where solitary men revere another I

steadied by darkness folding
I see small men marching
rattling and whining

looking for a dark leader

night is an open window
that I often find to my high liking
every time I am the one
to conclude the day

~

sold by infamous men marching
with drenched wrist watch salesmen
in cauldrons boiling with greed's ire
I must bind the seldom to the I sky
where something is no more

before all folds into thin air
time will yet be unforeseen
by petty coin collectors
reigning with inherit insolence

rude to the very core of us all
staring into the broken shadows

I see the why falling
like a lost cause into invisibility
dark trials of no avail Sunday
are no more than a yesterday
in a grey mind matter
banks never considered

not ceremoniously
nor for the sake of a decency

glorious madmen bleed dark I
sluggish tissue stains
wet sand wave waiting in awe
grained by doomed drums of war
the semi-precious stone with a sharp cut
undermines untamed intentions
of the mono psychopath I
deeming importance to be all
a dead speaker need

~

time is a staple gun
ticking like atoms in advance
serenity is a call girl
doing time for dark men I
sap is a vernal thing
running with silly messages
from thaw to twig
in days to come

salamander worm and frog
the mud is in a wondrous bed
with the seasonal change
a thaw that ripens

die for me
bury all I am not
under forest trees
nodding to the sunshine

salmon and trout is jumping
sex is a known contingency

calling for horny emergency procedure
and more sweetened coffee

I am old pipe passed to my peer
hot smoke behind tinted glass
rolls that can turn darkness into I
simplicity in a base view I

~

seaward sailor seaward
rocky shores bend like lovers
in a naked rain trembling

the beckoning rides the tide
like a dream in a stream
turned backward

fencing for the right to wander
illusive realms of sleep
I find distilleries among the stars

starship engines roar
with the power of a thousand suns
pounding frailty with fire

there are women calling to the sea
roaring like mama Africa
on Arabic radio stations

lost in the tales of an old man
I taste serendipity
in single malt and dark brew

running for office
I looked for different words
to prolong the day

vernal equinox
hackney hearse echoes
the ceremonious sing song
it is a short span indeed
between the invite
and the needs of the ones

I saw a male mallard today
why must day turn
into night

~

I am manmade devil
demanding nothing but blood
in blood's dead domain
I see a paradise erected for the dim

by the unintelligent
reeking with deeds of hate

I smell spring rotting into indifference
trees pleading in crowded airports
and morning subways

I see justification like a fig burning
a delirious vision so mad
people will die for it

to kill for a dream so terrible
where old men talk dirty
wanking through the empty night

~

there are different ways
one can spill content
into a metaphor
make a point even if
there isn't one

~

the color of night bursting into bed
pleads with forgetfulness
just to find enough space to roam

~

sleepy bright afternoon a breath
steadied by Spring in trees
shuddering in shadows creeping with the
worst
a rummage through the thawing of the earth
songs of silence move in the last rays
of solitude dancing with a fools crown
there are men stuttering on stilts
law men abiding their turn at the gap
unseen blankets smoldering unseen fires
hate is not even an insect nor a coiled thing
more a self-inflicted bleeding
a dead fly in your throat

there are rats in the fliers
daring man to sleep dead end sleep
with whiskers and heart dark and straight
like a liver strung high on fire
there is a bold panic
among the glistening hoarders

of dead end dreams of men
drooling repetitively in any wind
not knowing the difference
between fools dawn and a grave
evaporating hissing
stealing without touching

~

steady hand holds day
shooting like a star
through all history
and the silent spaces
in between

I hold you a while
I love
the way you smell
the way your skin meets
my longing

stream me not by the sea
wear me like a brooch
pinned to your skin
rolling like a tidal wave
to a final shore

~

sorted by the intimidating
scolded by the almost dead
wired to the aching
I see no folding
into ditches burning
I am no cluster of emotion
no antidote against forgetting
yet constantly sinking
into the unknown I am
scraping toilet walls
running with fever
where there is no tomorrow
driving Italian racing cars
over money borders
where Islamic war lovers
tick with bombs
close to mother at home

sorted by mere mortals
done for in times all splintered
in times of no serious say so
I find two in a skirmish
to be three in an altar piece
where loaded with rich man's lies
the iconic simplicity is cluttered with sheep
and any silly reason to collect on Sunday
there are no gilded limbs
one can join at the hip
no excuse of another day

we are only here today
no more

~

vernal to the bony bed of I
lingering in dairy wombs
where winds will not suffice
there will be an uprising
with voices rattling of death
finally will be the pale and stiff
charmed to the teeth in caves
with I man and wasteland talking
I is of no consequence here
to wrecks in shadow wars dying
dark crayfish crawl in corporate men
bullies anyone for the sake of a clean bed

~

it is not of today sanctioned
waves of yesterday roll
with the answers I am

pale hands bouncing
taut skin's resurrection
in a soft beat turning

shadow draft bleeding
there is no consolation
with old age

~

steeped in tales of no more
dampened and paid for
by wealthy fools and chance

I place my final bet
on number eleven

there are cracks in the slip up
loads of confirmation
in the arms of spiderlike men
dying to take your temperature
with them back to hell

sallow moon eaten by cows
stars outlawed by the state of Kansas
weed is for men of lesser ambition
tea for those with social skills
a blue sky is just a blue sky

~

I in I love you weeps in why
standing by a sullen shore
dipping tardiness in crystal water

it is getting late my love
the cool spring night in my arms
drips like a melting kind of good bye

dance red coat boot and tail
there are so many stories in our lives
images that fade with the wind

there are summer days
never promised
and yet so full of yearning

there is a goodbye lingering
in the heat of the sun
in the bold garden scent

~

so gentle this wind
this solitude
where I long for you

"serendipity" you whispered
"be the water
you came from"

the cherry trees are in bloom
the garden yields
to the vernal sky above

~

night is a time to forget
the many hidden sorrows
flowing in line not to regret

deep chasms gape and grin
over all lost tomorrows
where I have never been

~

solemnity in the blink of today
rushes into a new history
of pale bones and dirt
I saw you dance in the light
enhanced by the short of it
collecting all dues in I goodbye

serenity is a fast dare undoing
the allotted and the rolling
a love any man can muster

I saw you folding sheets of light
carrying the final stone to rest
like a badge of impossible honor

~

slow tidal agreements flow
like tempestuous dares
just before the coming of war

these locusts are not mine
this dark plague of light's refusal
I will not mourn the death of a child by fire

there are no deities in death
no solemn welcome
when the lights go out

dark waves roll with sharp teeth
boats that will not last the night
will sink like they should

there is a demon in the water
there is a demon on land
beheading decency with numbers

~

walking in the wake of this world
one might find oneself in a bind
there's no remedy for that
cascading colors of spidery nights
seduce you time and again
with promises of forever and ever

this profound love I feel I know
so brief ephemeral and sweet
it will break my heart to die
to say good bye before the canvas
leaving all the unwritten
on the cemetery of final silence

~

there is too much silence these days
too much nothing more
to go with the rest of it

we should be many by now
with our hands and tongues
relentlessly in protest against
foul gutter prophets preaching

hate was never in the original script
was never meant to have a purpose
in the survival of the evolved

dairy trains roll across the waste land
daring the pale hobo
dangling above the cattle
making butter with hungry words

~

with one hand dead to the tenderness
we all agreed upon when young
we swarm at best
declaring war and making food

we do not dance to ancient flutes
we do not polish the floor

with our need to shine
we walk the spidery walk to a halt

dare me not on a Sunday morning
all dreamed up like a boat on a river
steamed and ready to boogie
with the best of us

~

yielding to the shadow of repetition
I pity he who counts his victories
by the stricken hour

the importance of running
with cruelty and hate
resounds in the psychotic prayers
of any dull religion

I pity any man afraid of dying
feeding his furnace with small coins
and hollow lacerations

~

I am the suspect one
facing lost floor disdain
crevices will open because they can

so much agony in the I eye
so many sullen goodbyes
the solid of it all will not go
because I will not

I am totaled and sea mad falling
rakishly brash and brave to the bone

waves full of salty tears break
on a dark sullen winter beaches
it is only I in a mood

~

I am the sudden aftermath
the desperate interlude
the way I write

a tale taller than I
moves slow Sunday
into another room

I find terminology of no use
importance is fettered
and I am not

~

stealth is a Stabat Mater
hiding at busy street corners
never revealing her intentions
dodging swords and tar
unfeathering the solemnity
of short landscapes
beneath any cobbled street

fire brigades line up
just to set an example
men in top hats flip coins
just to make sure

sterile indigestion is a no no
dancing at the top of I
is so much more fun

~

dare is another word
for letting your hair down

I can hear you now
even as you face the mirror

rubble at the edge of town
preachers groping for young boys
singing like angels
in a market closet choir

dreams of common decency
whirl like a late night dervish
in a glass of piña colada with ice
constantly melting

there's no remedy
for a lack of empathy
there's no way around
careless complacency

~

dare me you fed up with feathery fire
with love and fierce flames birthed
at the dip of dark star turning you

mass me not into mercury graves
where old tradition run with clocks
into why with a grin and fake churches

sun dials will run for president
only in the summer
in the aftermath of all said and done

~

repetitiously and still in vane
dogs congregate where men
reside in small numbers
where one never can be two

dereliction is a wart
a blemish on the pale skin of decency
black men toil in mines just to see minerals
land in the hands of others

there is a sandy song in the desert
singing of mountains far away
of pure water rippling under stones
in a place called Viridian

~

I am the solidity
of winter days
frozen like low lakes
with grey ice
above all sluggish fish
fronting dark water
in spite of the market

~

no reason to run
eons of mute repetition
out of town

a street has no name
if abandoned
a square can be shunned

squirreled and doved
with even more snow
just to make sure

a fast breathing sky
leaves event horizon derelict
in a single fold of darkness

~

"seaward" she said pointing
one hand beckoning
"streamlined and polished
by relentless tides"
she looked funny
in a mushroom sort of way
constantly folding her Tarot cards

years later when we met
she said "waves worry me
and the water we cannot hear
will not be the end of it"
I left her by a lamp post rolling
when my own ending
gave birth to a dead squid cooking

phosphorous nights when jellyfish gleam
seem to find me pending between poems
and all that one can muster in a here to be here
"there is no final blessing
it is all so human"
she dived into lands unplucked
by fools of believing

~

these keys unlock more secretes of I
when wired to slow beast bone dancing
in a celestial corpse style
there one can dare the salmons to jump
snails move slower those days
I am the antithesis of more
and much more than the less of it

small men congregate continuously
in hollow shadows of old religion
where sword and blunt spear
keep the righteous in line
they think fall out is in check
they dream of more
than they can understand

sterility is hate's true intention
sworn like a dark feather dying
for a sooty chimney hat
stuck with forever with a dice
leaning against my forehead
I rest in a cod's watery silence
silently dividing the sea

~

reverberating in the grey
of a bleak winter's day

a bird looked at me
through the cold of a thin drizzle
running from a roof tile shine

I need to stretch a different wire
to jump up and down while
listening to the radio

where are all my friends
the people I should've met

wrought like a warm hand
stretched before the sketch
of bare trees against a lead sky
that will say no more
than it has to

in that way I will sing my eyes
worming my dreams into boots
that will not march
there is something about dreariness
in the silence of a cold rain

~

23 23 does not return your call
rolling knee joints to curved music
evaporating into a dissolving
a glue or a threshold to worlds

where a glance is no more than a glance
where ale taste better than dark wishes
more than a spoonful of love

ceremoniously I dive November
where tidings of I is more

than poor man's said-so
where I in a different walk along

dream of sea and more
than a soft kind of dying into water
without I goodbye
where I is brute continuity broken

steepled wired going hay
I finds I summarily
unwanted and further away
from all concerned
I dived vertically fronting wind
while you walked another score
venting streams in a different day
beating on dead drums with sonority

~

rolled into a dark chariot
an embryo of slow night falling

I dare you to find me harlot
hear me call to the birds

dark sky folds its time gone
while I on the other side
blend this windy crime investigation
with tales of a frozen tide
reckless night is a bending night
with boughs of dark sorrow
adrift in dark sky's slow rending
without a thought of tomorrow

~

it's not the Chinese
nor the Afghanis
it's the encounter
with the known universe
a sword with an edge to grind
that will squash the lot

it's not the Russians
nor the North Koreans
that will go the extra mile
to extinguish manmade nonsense
it's men staring at dead stars
men that will not go to the races

~

rapacious wolf grabs the world
by the wavelength and number of tiles
repeating its lust for blood
flock running with dead forefathers

still in line rocked and sued
for the rest of the day
the wolf ticks in a different way
just to stay out of close range

steepled dead and in a bad shape
wolf bleeds in malice on your carpet
stares snorts and prepares you
for a different approach

I am blind religion says he
that owns the script
that keeps you at long bay
and me at the helm

dream me not
I am the antithesis of all
you ever wanted
put a sail to

"leverage" someone shouted
from the dimmed galleries
"don't forget the I dying"
there are so many stories

~

there was a certain hush
a kind of sinister silence
religious men will die for

the evening dark was more
than crouching mistress hidden
beneath a waxing moon

her clock fading face
is a smear in the sky's eye
a lament with no tears

so many cultures
so many different stories
I hear a saz a darbuka

leniency she claimed
was hers and not of the kind
migrant birds crave

"a stride is but a foot long
a measurement that can be made
of anyone's mistake"

disparately and out of order
dragged into a we-be-it
focus finds its own shift of tale

"derelict dysfunctional and dying
I is dropped irony
lining up by the scaffold"

~

I a wafer in a church
heading for Christmas
with graves burning
yearning for fish and wine

delving is a pastime
for porcupines and brides
waiting for new gills
to make a difference at the ball

stained and left behind
charcoaled and chalked
one is always on a rebound
framing history with color

sleep me in my solemnity
as old music rolls
with a chilly draft of jellyfish
stuck in the wet sand

clear why turning into sky
resemble I face in disdain

roll wishful smile into
yesterday rambling today

there is a sculpture
standing by the whishing tree
a scooter waiting
by the end of sweet sixteen

~

derelict with a wooden bible
carved from the old back
of ordinary waves rolling in December
stranded knee deep in cold silt
fraught with one way streets
like a head full of wild hair
streamlined wired and waterpiped
I is just another shadow
dancing with old bones pending
in a night fraught with slow fireworks
surprised by the unending water
swirling like a pack of swans
just above your head
it is the night of both hands bending
the moment of accounting
for the all I can perceive
danced scrutinized and alive
in I in welcome done
at the far end of the table

~

flustering death I say
bind me and bind me not
to this world
where peculiar men gnaw
where I or not I
tread on frozen water rolling
descend cold chimneys
where the eye is a bone
calling ordinary men
for thin shadows
at the end of any notion

preachers will fall into the smell
of protuberant prayers rising
like hidden marsh gas
from the world of dead men
feeding the hungry soil
a bleak blasphemy
of the human kind
never ending
never apologizing
a taint a stain
a sort of longing for a self

~

when smoke rises sky to mind
time tends to bend days direction
to fit creatures that cannot speak

dainty little I burn brevity
in a whispered pipe in turn
dare the bear to dance unchained

I walk a dog to land a house
you can feed I low low
with down severity down

I hear rumored dragons mourn
in a thin paper once rolled
into a long winter breath

I will go down with music
and voices hanging laundry
on a wicked line for all to see

~

striped like a diary man on the run
I faked a farmer tap dancing at will
because the metric system
is wired that way

there are men on the move
concerns graver than death
roam through the labyrinth
afterbirth is not only I

daring night after dark night
to relinquish its hold
on new world demands
I walk the hall of more I

I am the late night tide
rolling slow motion sand
with heron and scallop singing
the heavy sigh song of life

~

rapacious day eats day
grey with old time's blues
in the gutter tonight
bleeding in poor consolation
to the sound of misery
squeezing darkness out of I

we met briefly by the counter
hoisting flags and smiling
we were introduced as torn winds
that were not borne

to find any final break comfort
where I do not care anymore

silenced into screams
suffocating
in halls of suicide bombers
where terror is just another death
by the moonless hand
the dead one

and there are governments
that condone extreme violence
invading any country
that has a new device
to detect white smoke
rising from the rich clergy

the righteous march
zealots wrap dynamite
around their young lives
the tick tock of the duped
ignites yet another market
burning dread into the night

~

the I winter eye running
with bowties and fireworks
over crispy ice shores I

where a dog's heart
may beat bark at a whiskey moon

the reckoning constantly calls you
with visions of a different I
damning all malicious darkness
into other tales told
where the shine does not why

dipped weaseled washed ashore
one man is all
this turning darkness needs
procuring tinder
whaled into good night

~

seldom by wavering water
seldom questioned for beds
serenity laughs like a comedian
high on ether or whispering

dead man's bed is downward
abandoned arid and arbitrary
like a needle in a ring of trees
or hung on a neck in time

stem me a another pint you fool
find me a feathering far out

where I am not totaled
because of you

revised cared for and nourished
one more death is consumed
just before breakfast
while there still was time

~

steepled by a church high on holy water
destined for the love of what water is
waves roll all over lost shores
deep in the I where the I in you stand

eternity is a day in total decay
never knowing where I actually I-begin
there is still time to reclaim birth
in an ordinary glass of beer

~

it is the night of all refusal
dimmed and lost
at the foothills of yesterday
weary with a strap on
like a hard imprint

testifying to winter dark
being irrevocable

stained stamped and bitten
where winter night is relentless
I signal to all I will miss
not with a pope's white smoke
but with a temporal ignition
rapidly turning any day
into grey ashes

~

do not salute devils dawn you fool
flawed by the immensity of useless death
solitary trees stretch in small men
catching fire behind the wheel
we are all intentions that steam and storm
lurking in a day's rolling aftermath
I smell sulphur in a rain of burning lime
hurry my dear hear me still dying
we must still walk across this old fear
and wild steeds will still hesitate
to ford where dread runs like dead water
and if someone asks you for a coin
run while you still can

this is only last of it
a tear in the last ray of the unformed

~

seriously
we are all alive
or planning our death

let's conject that
we do believe in morality
so we must kill

I do not like you
but I will build a house
on your property

cheap missiles suffice I'd say
or knifes at a fake border
high-rise is not a fruit

let's be human

~

I am the difference
between here
and what might be

the voice of stale night
rumbling into goodbye
before a babbling rabbit moon

we are dead trees talking
wind rustling things
that mark the passing of time

damn if I can be sure
is it a wave or a particle
or just total volatility

darkness talks in lost woods
running from small men
losing by the hour

there are times
when even the passing
holds no say

salutations to the still walking
to the dead strung like beads
across an opposite universe

there are terrains where one walks
in dark days with a face off
daring darkness with more wine

this life this you this I this nothing
a pale tram ride in a fading memory
a dream with no names running

you that yield to the flag
bonfired and rolled like joint
meant as a fuse

there are small men
crawling like sooty spiders
just to say boom

~

you could never hold me down
with your fierce fire folding lethargy
I knew your tempting water to well
you tried to snap me bold at night running
like a tree in full storm I bellowed

but you track stopped me dead
in time for poems to dye the world

lemmings walk into cliff absolution
trees go root wise to a communion with
yesterday
there is no time for fake funerals
with strange fruit in old trees

elementary is pure dereliction down
a translation of so much wrong
into a poke in the night

~

stair me high
beer me
Jung me here
where solution is mused
alcohol fired
and burning with dead drool

drive me not but still
brick wall me
into here dark certainty
with smoldering heritage caution
eyed with misunderstanding
shifting into empty space

tooled into a sad moon
almost hidden in goodbye I
where you fall in volatile ways
I see is the high I visible
in any winding bereavement
dancing fictitious breeze

totally wired with Finnegan
I sonorously signal

tear dreams with pale shreds
to make funny money from air
running to the end grave
just for the fun of it

~

strands of liquid copper
catching fire in the early sun
the old buildings break
under pink streaks of sky
streets roll with whole empires
under yet another rising sun
there's one futile questions to go

streams of dead said so
keep the rain in a new fashion
derelict beings howl
at the same in the water wild
I in the machine
will not hold my breath
if there's a sudden deluge

~

silt on my early foreplay I
where slipped is like an old diary
telling small tales

there is no way you can hear
ancient rock cracking time
like a walnut

danced with dynamite and froth
flawed like a Siberian tiger
in the tropics I with voice light
I dare the untold rest
to move out of the way
there are no toys left
serendipity holds no answer

~

there's a hidden creek
bubbling in day's aftermath
earth's rumbling tenants
wear shoes fit for a new war
falling from dark windows

it is time to be jolly
to let the shoe shine boys
circle you with their poor decency
rolling a finger fired longing
with birds turning hot ash

destiny is a logical must go there
unruly and chaotic it grasps
at the last will not executed yet

passing in absolute conclusion
with a tuliped birthday bouquet

a seldom spotted day unread by most
run for its existence and a daily spin
where wealth is a ship on murky waters
circumcised just to make sure
those introduced to myth will pay

good night runs like a wild guess
screaming ferns and feathered dogs
to the herons in clam-coves dashing
with poignant silt dying for air
or a last glimpse of why the fuzz

detoured derailed detracted
one fell in a forward somersault
daring late tide to turn vehicular
and be gone for good

drivel smokes a fake joint
in a short say so undermining
sooty ecology wheezing
for being outlawed

I dreamed of a different world
where beef is not food
where a sacrifice
never entails an altar

I steeped in dead churches
of such a liquid beauty
that the one hollering
finds no relieve red doors

serpentines whirl roads
into thoughts into fast food
where wild men decide
the way of the world

a sudden song on the radio
a few lines of a poem drifting
through yet another summer
lifting the skirt of the wind

~

I am surrounded by nurses
gasping like
fish deprived of water
worms stuck in tiny tunnels
during the heavy rain

I am foretold
omnipresent
exhaled into this world
like mist on a glass
of aged wine

dreams we are
a collective madness
bouncing up and down
steepled and done for
by the continuity

when I saw you I knew
the rest would follow
pleasantly and stolen
from the orchards where men
tend to eat themselves

~

you are so full of pictures
kaleidoscopic images
flittering on naked skin
you are such an ocean
a cod dreaming of the Atlantic

you are so illustrated
so well versed and picture smart
that rare ideas seem petty
compared to the inherit tattoos
and all raw facts

I see air plummeting fast
as your body time fails
getting on terms with erasure

is not an option to run and sleep
it's a bloody fact

~

the philosopher's breath
runs like dead water from a faucet
herons pray for images in the bathroom
with a cockled brain for breakfast

there are dragons in the South
pleading with the bishops
for a go at the children at school
the white smoke was never real

suddenness is a ripened hare
jumping for the hell of it
chlorophyll turns into heat
there are baskets made for all

~

dipped into sonic rates
of a phosphorous fraud
serendipity sticks it to the ducks
in bleak afternoon fading slow
with specks of dark silver
flittering in the old way

there is a message here somewhere
where night is a capsule of white dust
we can still survive
the first of the horsemen
but there is no more
after the first death

~

diaries are on the run
the blood of the innocent
run thick and grey
in the leave me not veins
the unholy I will not kill you
for looking at my mother

this is the day of dark reckoning
says he with the biggest gun

slow to wake me up
finds the day shredded
by a Muslim suicide squad

elements of sharp incision
are inserted into putrid flesh
there is no other one

I can see no growth
day pollutes night
cream curdles and shrink away

street children starve
goes to sleep with glue
lives outside the law

~

solemnly and with no shadow
cast across silent surgeon's table
day submits it all to night

remembering the thoughtfulness
wind talks to frozen pond
dog will not eat dog

no epiphany congregates here
where words are like solitary tools
of dark manmade destruction

sleepy follow makes no difference
do not care is a sleep drug
administered by the brown shirts

deep end is a gullible tale at the close
where observation turns
into a hasty hole in the ground

~

I dance into dizzy oblivion
lobotomized while in deep sleep
there is no end to all erratic innuendos
mumbled in the totalled pews
on a Monday morning

it drizzled and fizzled and died
the first clock was made out of tin
there is no heritage in words
no genetic spiral in the silence
between the rolling of waves

~

the young ones
do not know

dying
dying

the dogs
our neighbours
dying

a sweet smile
can hide
the fact

a kiss
can erase it
for a day maybe
or two

I am so in love
with
being alive

I
can suppress
the inevitable

but I am dying

~

serene like fish in a tank
loaded with a luminous shining
I like guns and gun powder versified
finds myself in a bind
moralized and limed in bed
during another raid

lasting for a full hour
imploding with memories
of early 1940
groping for money
and territory
or just the book of debts
over those
that will have to pay

blue dragons
claw deep into the flesh
of those
that dig for gold

men will die
there will be a new opium war
the hash men will ride again
shining sword in hand

infidels will be robbed
by the mystery mistaken
for a fish in the water
that preceded us

~

dare runs like a shoal of fish
in a barrel of fun for the privileged
dogs run like beer in bars

where fur is a reason for morons
to dig deep into empty pockets

weather is always on the run
serendipity and ubiquity
play on the same team

night is not really a parent
not even a distant relation

rhythm is a fast day's mystery
downloading all immediacy
into the hard drive of I
turning all hands-on into true labour
dancing in a rippling goodbye

sworn to secrecy short of loss
worn like an ancient symbol
rolled into high night rolling
where mushroom bleat
on brevity's brittle altar boy

stooled fingered and loaded
I do not fool around with pronouns
they are we too
dash why not dash
we are the last of these years
to be seen ever

when the loaded brush
touched the canvas
the colour came alive
pleading with presence
for eyes in I

I am the flute that hesitates
the finger stayed
the note that will not go
before air finally talks
in time exhaled

~

white winter tales of burden
flee days of bright thunder
a sudden wisp of vastness
opens like a tin of tuna in the sun

there is a certain distance
between the I and the world
there are men constantly in love
with the machine that feeds them

there are politicians claiming
more funds for the plenty
goggles for the upper class
beaches in the sun for all with money

dark tales of wonder
walk in invisible shoes
there are men who will claim
and die for a free surface

~

there's a bright hole in the sky
where our dreams are fed
with the hope of more
than a shovel and a salute

stars are no better
swirling on vast straws
cast into the observed void
for no reason at all

I will not listen to dead voices
wait for ordinary bushes
to catch fire and burn bright
I am not special

say is there a heaven for dogs
for cats and old turtles
where they truly can hear
their master calling

this day turning bold
winking with one eye

to the settlement of all dying
is all we have

~

stigmatized and driven into misery
run out of town by the do-gooders
with a silent cry of winter tears
shedding cold dreams
never freezing why

begging for a last meal dying
on the back of a harsh world lying
money keeps on waging war
bombing silence into oblivion

a coin with a smile a distant hope reeling
a rag doll with a face of despair
banned from all progress
returned to the tarp in the woods

the lottery of birth is prejudicial
there's a biased crew
so cynical that sheep fart
in halls wallpapered with money

~

walking umbrella styled
perceived as a slow train coming
like a freight rain running
but not today
not today I say not today
I will never care for postures
or a fancy swaggers
stiff like blunt daggers saying
will you walk to the edge with me
holding on to my future
with your eyes only

it was a radio severing track
one could hear cluck
from a here shore where luck
has nothing to do with rest of it
hammers beat on bad weather
that will come creeping
down the aisle with green drapes
and water will return from ice
in a dance we cannot see
and a good night will still be
a child put in bed

~

pierced like a wind I am
folding sleepy sparrows
into good night

distanced by the final call
like a gull above the sea
I cry for more beer

standing by your side
I see a belled belonging move
into a different light

I can almost touch
this longing that we are
streamed and long lost

steep me not nor ever again
ravished is a fatal move
succulent and dying dying dying

~

stolen into oblivion on a night
remedy calls for no more
here rouge bands are aided with silicon
and a dash of white lemon skin
in an echo of a slave trade not gone

resources are like paid tools
moving on command
a multitude of strings
at the hands of a puppet master

driving everyone to the market
on Bank holiday Sunday

the bus drivers are on strike
the fishermen loiter en masse
at the top of the quay stairs
just for the hell of it

Maggie won't let no be the answer
relies on broad shoulders
just to forget the wet laundry
and dead men walking on record
in single bars at dawn

stumped by weather
folding winds
just for the hell of it
it is the night you must be
or just one more

~

I am the unfolder
the untold
amongst the weary
and
the almost dead

I've read
that bold men
and
unscrupulous women
dare the rest

so far
no one survived
to tell the rest of the story
migrants struggle
my mother
is a dying mother

rather is a concept
embraced
by the petrified
salt is a must
amongst the dead
winds
can be pierced

there is a certain
what ever
reading Tarot and I Ching
waking up
in different cities
just to ascertain
winds do not matter

love me here that I am
so I don't need to make bail
or brand your family
breeding endlessly
for the sake of
the killer tree embroidering
skulls in circles

~

unsteady by any account
where hands and charts waver slow
by the blow by the minute and the show
in the coming of dark snow

cremated by the marching night
beaten by dormant anger death no fight
strides are white just to make sure
one will not stay upright for ever

rampant ice on fire parades
with one hand on the socket
the other on the final switch
there's a lullaby in my pocket

Green Peter walks in dreams
with eyes for joy exhaled pale

she sleeps like a new horizon
a wreath of roses across the sea

eyes stolen from the Mayflower
run secretly for mayor
in the deep dark town I will

variety rolled the final dice
steeds died and I was fed with barley
we all ran for office

coffers turn into sediment
soil is a name
we should get used to

streamed into bruised clergy
white collars that prey
on small children

a man with one leg
is just that
no need for puppeteers

~

driven
by default
in this chisel wind
run out

of simmering protest
by default

flaked
fortified and alone
by default

there is no I
moving the air
as I speak

thin smoke
has nothing to do with
papal election

there is a fake tear
in the sky
fooling the fools

just to make sure
there were free remedies
on the sidewalk

one walks alone
I have I
this is not real

it is I dancing train and tracked
into yesterday's never

seen by the few left dancing
that will die in time

severe distant and so forlorn
remedies turn to rhythm
just to find more abandoned shoes
and an elastic evil

~

opulence rides in a stretch Lincoln
soaked in a smell of red oranges
moist with green tea

feudal masters don't bleed
nailing carpenters
to the wooden floor

the ravished look for hammers
can in turn be used
to make food for the poor

a rhythm on the radio
pleads with small drums
and a full orchestra squirming
for a chance at the table
there at flowers
at the top of every new score

there are so many turns
mapped and spoiled by fools

there is a tambourine tree
at the end of my street
where one can get a freebie
just for turning up

there is no substitute
for the real McCoy
as I run up and down the street
looking for the man

~

remedies of old age
fall like a winter's rain pounding
turning life's hard page
like a butterfly in pain shrivels

drearily done is long gone
semiotic preferences
fail to respond
day will be no more

reverence is a sugar cunt
solemnity is a dead bird
sold by Cleese
for the sake of a laugh

terrible and for sale
I find detergent reasons
not to inhale what I
never meant to be

rapacious man devolves
where I cannot flow
tomorrow's ice and ire
is all gone

~

who will not run from blind men
operating without consent
in theatres of quenched mercy
who will not flee markets
where blind hate madly ignites
a dark dog prophecy

there are men dying to kill you
exposing children to pointless murder
there are transparent women
kept like horny men's trophies
on broken mantelpieces
there's more to ember than loss

stern does not play ball at midnight
firm goes religious at any time
hand in hand they dare

the only end to burst out
like a ring of fire
knocking on every door

~

stern amongst the perished
loathing all labour
failing to appear unfurnished
one leaves it all
to the other one

semblance is a failure
when it appears in court
driven is an adjective
used amongst the ones
born and street danced into full stop

remedies are feeble
beer is for the masses
but no mass
can make up for the rape
of young choir boys
or bitter nuns punishing
pregnant girls

there are certain values
or rather

there are certain ways
of understanding
the way one perceives
what really goes on
when no bribe is attached

leverage is a blunt instrument
daft goes a long way
when nights mistress
is what many can appreciate
or let be
direction means more beer
or a simple smile

~

fear not wrath wrought
like carved timber
around your intention

dance not to the sound
of the deadly dime
collect no special favour

striped and skin-snaked
like in the ol' myth
why is still not an apple

craved in still water reunion
like oysters or slow trout
one must be at large

~

steadily I say walk no more
there are armies of much lo
and all kinds of behold
coming your solitary way

in a hot dessert one can hear
whispering scorpions
move like sharp fish under ice
singing slow perception

rhubarbed into a stricken tomorrow
silenced with tons of stale bread
and a dash of dark discord
I render this illusive place I am
there are parrots in the machinery
strange patterns dark suits
undoing what cheap may adopt
with notes of a final despair

~

eloped into dark silence of day
one finds no way to play
or secretly stay
there is nothing more to say

silence is so abandoned
hate frames the locked door
wistfulness drives forged nails
into any observation

there's no law
that says
one man cannot
be more than one man

reclusiveness fortifies silence
there are all kinds of runners at large
we must all solidify this time
in a head on refusal

nurses bend and chant
lost in dictionaries
riding the one train
going home

dialled and received
birds call for any day
to increase the waxing light
and any winged joy

I saw you flittering
in a late light wind
of early Mars
brushing against my kin

~

steep like a promise of spring
you rushed into me
holding high for low
presenting all your evidence
to the lower courts

birds follow you
winds can say your name
sorority of youth
fends for a right to forget you
yet you die every day
slept in a fever stable
with snorting steeds
pounding at the stalls
driving nails into raw flesh
I looked for you again

by a brook I used to dream
words gathered
just to make sure time
still was
a few more days

~

serpents swirl with the coming
of more snow or just one more day
limpid I neatly fold old light
into mysteries of more and same
there is a fine line drawn
between the living
and the feeble door knockers
barefoot crying a frosty farewell

weighed down by day's anchor
sleeping in forgetfulness
dragged and skinned
by the few that owes almost everything
piled into dark caves - no reason
greed is a powerful tool
amongst the possessively challenged

lives constantly flicker and die
generating more gold
to the preying dragons
not even in sleep is there justice
small men keep marching
just for the hell of it
lesser men look the other way
it's all about the Sumerian math

~

dredged by all accounts
a hoof print a tail behind a tree
a smell of raw earth
making us ready for the day

there are certain movements
composers tend to find
just before vernal equinox
rolls with thunder

resemblance is not a fact
one should give much importance
look for invisibility
moving one day into the other

~

dairy mothers lactate in vain
crap fathers survive in pubs
there are children in dire need
of more parenting

who will deep fry the fish
who will see to it
that chips are orderly arranged
before the march of the callous

serenity walks barefoot through I
no knickers needed today
the want of us all
is just a foolish turn of event

sails and rudders whisper
keels plough the earth
no one will ever beat
a fake truth confession out of you

dreamers are pioneers
wandering grey margins
that never will come
or amount to anything

streams of bright possibilities
bubble in these lost children water
where fountainheads call for a rerun
I am but an eye

streamed dying horrified
by the final emptiness
love has nothing to do with
bacteria going party wild

~

stern the sand beaten
by dark waves so pungent
salt seaweed jellyfish
dares death to roll like a wave
ripple and cry
from the ocean's lung

daffodilled lured
into a new kingdom coming
man beast in his perquisite place
finds air thick with a score
pinned to the pale petaled sky
with only a few words to go

~

sandpiped to the full extent of I
seen with waves of inner emptiness
I roll like a joint at dawn's calling

three lines in a row
three ways of moving a brush
across the white space of I

sullen groomed and in fear
one man finds himself
at war with all of existence

drenched in a breath of water
he gasps for fire
there is still hope for the clandestine

determined like a dead fish
diluted down
like cheap bourbon

I see I as water ship down
flooded with the pages an old book
or the unholy scripture

no need to hold hands
watch the sunset
glowing with pollution

three lines in a row
in a certain wind in a day that I
can move as I please

this is what I am
this is what life allows
in days of suddenness

~

cascades fall in memory line
folding yesterdays
into neat bundles of children

carrying the coming of more war
with the selling of more flags
cascades spume with a brutal force
lavishing expressions in days
of hate and scorn

whispered into different days
one finds himself spurned
with the outcome
of yet another cold night
there are trees in conversation
mills running wild
just for the sake of doing it

soon the desperate will set fire
to the old sarcophagus
the last of their burning money
will feed the unforgiving waves
with dark end shadows finally sinking
silently into the I
never finding peace at the end

~

a turn of the rain
sunshine breaking furniture
just for the sake
of old people surviving

on their own
with time diving deep

selective
I say
mariners to go
mama
say something else
sugar
is just not enough

remembering
old times
hung up on wine
too pale to walk the line
I set fire
to perception
running for presidency

lavished to the bone
sold for more money
than I can pay for
remembered at times
in caves where the weird
brew their own songs

when the steel casket reunion
fails to reconcile
with the dead and the lost
dreams will be a luxury

lost on the living
wise men will look for a toilet

~

to all voices that flow
there is a wind in trees
tantalizing gossip
wild tales and Saturn
spinning madly
when we don't look

to all men and women
possessing letters
that hold on to sanity
with images and sounds
where we all are
madly in love with I

this is just another day
where we can cease
with mindless absorption
the misery cat will run for its life
on a lettered cold beach
backstage

~

dipping my stale bread
in your unholy chalice
I beg you disagree
but it makes no difference
whether you approve
or not

funny mushrooms
shoot like bright stars
from a molten earth running
ready to set to the coastal sky
on fire with hands begging
grabbing for another day

reverberate you moon
amongst temporal gems
shine madly and full
above the realms of refuse
rolling to fast music of tall men
kneeling under a heavy hair do

sailors on watery ways run for money
mice and mucus flee bars
that melt in a dark fire
where murky altars reverberate
where one is sold for two more
no one can make a difference

remember the I folding
dirty laundry hanging in the wind

for the sake of being visible
in a time of constant burden
I do remember the chaos
that shaped the curved beaches
the mothers that wept for more

~

I see doubters in a late night sky
worried faces that roll
while running for office
in countries where dark flags
unfurl on any given day
ruled by the unfair

selected and unruled
we the few
crawl in solitude
for the sake of no war
no killing no hate
we reject indifference

steeped in still back water
where weary men run for cover
where tactile bombs
fall from skinny skies
where white rabbits run
we will not worry about time

streamed and silently crying
I see your need to grasp
and understand
the madness of these dervish times

the spitting image of loitering men
in an oyster's dream

I see the dull I see the shaved
there's a Buddhist calamity
a contingency with nothing to say
breathing heavily
in white man's weary day
reeling just for the sake of it

~

derelict on a floor to floor basis
where memories float
muddy in cold trenches
dug much to early
to amount to another war
I settle with you

it is still early spring
unexploded mines
ruminate in a pale sun
witches congregate

with druids and drunkards
in forgotten parks

on the pale side of the Bowery
with all its cheap dresses
blowing in the East River wind
there is a silent agreement
and a loud whisper for ransom

~

I see white men folding water
wild washing women daring winds
in a new round of survival
measly powers to be congregates
in caves chiselled by the dead

hear Latino rhythms breathing fire
into the hot air of a constant summer
the music multiplies a forgetfulness
through poor arid villages
where a meal really is a big thing

stale mate moves in the dark of the night
old tree trunks feed the green moss
there is no meaning to all this
just remember to pay your bills
and feed the hungry bed

you think you are James Dean in jeans
giving hand-outs to the needy
gained at low speed on Lower East Side
where myths and weird movies congregate
for the sake of making a president

~

a sullen rain walks
under a silent sunshine
tip toeing high above
the luminous clouds

there's a man with no socks
a child burning
in a lost city dream
birds that commit no crime

whispered into tomorrow
in a two-legged song
redeeming all silence
I find no shame or brevity

care for me here beloved
care for me not
there are no different days
just the one

~

to Frédéric

how long will this love echo
bright with memories
and colours
bleeding into the rising rock
of a new tomorrow

no regrets no tears dry
hard almost mummified
I in the mystery of I
find observation
no longer possible

softly talking back
running for a new collection
where I can roll any wind
into histories embedded for ever
I do remember

~

danced into a new day
why walked a mile
just to make sure
no one was following him

the lake shuddered and shifted
the ice was gone
the sky gave a shivering blue
back to the mystery

the so and so followed suit
in its own fashion
there were no sexy maids
hiding in the woods

rising above the trees
birds find air to their liking
there are dark kings
running for power in the district

suddenly there is a word
that says it all
flowing like a wind
with a mission

there are men
that will boil dogs alive
there are days
you don't want to be

diluted days of no real worth
plague the coming of he

who will chat you up
with a bunch of old stories
and cheap wine in a paper cup

restless I mould my time
again and again
tearing at the loose fabric
men tend to get lost in
doing their thing

it's so great to exhale
molecular air
and still retain a sense
of a timed ride
on the back of a dragon

Gilgamesh was renamed
all the ancient floods
became one significant one
some blame it
on the extra-terrestrials

a fig or a bay leaf
cannot begin to compare
with ayahuasca or cactus
common fly agaric
or the herbal influence
there is a shaman in my pond
there is a shaman in my tree
I need to feed the wind

and gain access to the tangible
the wet earth calls

~

I God light dark fires
not knowing what flame
can burn what salient say so
upon streets happening

grief is a manmade monster
daring decency
to race for more sympathy
while war still is raging

dependency is a city
fed in a mindless city play
by dark worshippers
turning furious tragedy to night

the Doppler effect
is all about sound and perception
a religious man cannot be
in iridescence

a different city met the still I
rolling through empty streets
shrugging ash and blood
doing time for reason at all

~

a full moon fastened
like a pin to the dark blue sky
see the purple birch

~

meek men shall go
riding the tail of fairy virgins
to a place of pure madness

spring will roll with tiny bells
in a garden to come
toads will return to the pond

there are doors and there is silence
whispers tend to find percussion
at the end of the gathering

while closing the end of day
I see a homeless dermatologist
move across the known diary
written by the still dead
and their so-called matter nots

driven like a million rusty nails
into the nerve of yesterday

a doodled forest shrinking like age
I sink into the hot asphalt
like salt in a burning wound

smouldered swept and sundered
danced into such a warped day
that one cannot dispute the sound
of ten thousand lonely hearts
beating in the mortuary muscle

wormed gone and deactivated
surreal and warbled like a foetus
not even scars can feed
at long bay's what's up dude
it is time to let go

~

garbled into oblivion
where why never finds an ear
no one has ever read a book

solemnity is an old remnant of I
from times of nothing to say
to a prayer at the drop of the coming

holster your herbal shots cowboy
move across the known garden you
like a known fiend on a green holiday bus

it is only I that can bleed in navy blue
across these clear cerulean skies
where secrets are so obvious

~

there is poetry in the sun down
in the evening down
collecting coins from the masses
leaping over dead dragons
shouldering protective fires running
just to make it through the night

dare any fickle day to smile at dawn
where planning is impossible
where all great minds pauses in mid-air
where I will call a dream a spade
where the rest of us will still die in vain

~

there's a broken woman in my kitchen
demanding immediate entrance to my head
without coherence or humility
daring all of us with brash news
and strange tales of urgency and death by
drugs

it's just another day with warbled claims
who are we to tell the difference
between a narcissistic protuberance bulging
and dark desires intent to rule us all
with fear and intimidation

there is a kind of solitude in observance
or perhaps it is a kind of waiting
for lonely men to burn with told time
folding ordinary realities
into small bundles of forgetfulness

sedimentary rivers have no disdain
for he who retains a certain kind
of tellable truism

hand carved yet sold for a tiny pittance
on a market undone and gone
long before the selling of the she stung

I leave no matter unturned
darkness will not dictate the moment
when I come to the point
that being nice in a malicious rain
will make no difference

~

"dare me tomorrow" she said
her big eyes rolling day into dusk
"find a way to halt
the onslaught of lesser men"

it was a harsh command
I knew I had to follow
like night into next morning

"what do you see" she asked me
"is there anything worth saving?"

I knew she was serious
aiming for another chapter
of the on-going

I could hear the organ player
grind by the late-night mirror

"walk with me" she said

suddenly I was kind of afraid
to join or agree

"solemnity is a book
of weird tales
with testimonies of the living"

I was finally left
between the aim and the end

~

stemmed and steepled
launched towards the dark sky
like a juggling ball halting in mid-air
or a flying sofa in the Middle East
surrealistic like clocks melting
on the weird tail of Robin Hood

I say this to my defence:
"there are no ants

or funny bones
at the end of why I care"

strange is a juicy mandarin
in love with the device
that will squeeze it

the I will fall
like a final curtain

~

streamed like a fast car
racing for glory
on the streets of Monaco
a demented wind

crashing into open windows
slashing at the why daft
the mislead will not follow me

derelict I am at this point
drooling at the thought of more
beneath a final sky
there's no escape no direction home
no appealing authority will take my
complaint
so what else is new
there is a suddenness to it all
tremendous is the privilege
I claim to be all mine
with the I am and the rest
of the wrongly circumcised
the ones with no hair
the meek and the psychotic
they all need air

late night was all tenderness
a glimpse into the I will go
where I can find a last connection
my two-timed observation
is the argument that I constantly am
at all times of the day
sleep me then and let me go

~

walking down these late days
with one foot in the sky
the other in broken
singing in my guns like fireflies
at the break of night

there's no direction left
just a notion of speed
days are ticking bombs

in a game of birthdays
constantly running past us

dereliction is the final trap
carrying no promises
in its old eye wheezing
a tired and sore back talks to you
supple is no more

spring never was a promise
of a mystic presence
that will redeem all days
there's a new calendar now
where I am not

~

last man turning evening
is a rash residue

a salt birds will shun
I run for cover
on streets dark with war

men will congregate in rooms
drawing charts of troop movements
running through the motion
of not caring for the other
there is no going back
whispered into tomorrow
one folds into two
with one hand only
there will be another death
by fire and dark fear

old man weeps in ale
dares the rest to follow him
usage is one key
to understand the short of it
counting the wear of days

~

serve the drum beat waves
down the great morning to next day
revel in the glory of tides
running from birth to the golden years
unchained the salty air
the coming of days in sweet streams

subtle and grand
with the inherit inspiration
of tales and miles of running
with all possible answers

rebel in the untimed machine
spinning further from the reason why
calling in the money-making air
taking all bets of the table
for the sake of a seat by the soup
a peak at the eating of the end game
sudden highlights and cow maids
talking to blue men with flutes
there is so much laughter
in life's curved mirror

wired high and having nowhere to go
salmon fall deep into the coming
of more Sargasso and seaweed forests
driving the chartered breed
far into a watery motion
seagulled into yes morning yes
screamed and cleansed
I water my skyline
with tales of tall kingdoms
that have no end
with dunes of no relevance

~

suddenness is a cup
of afternoon tea
a few notches on a gun
meant for those of a lesser faith
subtlety is a mollusc

a mussel on a winter shore
contracted and so sleepy

waves we are
foam and slow motion
rolling over wet sand
daring the rising tide
into pages of circumstance
why is not a question
it is a reason

~

my printer is out of ink
birds flitter and butterflies flutter
there's no telling
where I actually begin
and you end

dare the coming with hope
dare the falling to stop
dare tomorrow

not to come around
if you dare

there is a mad person
running around
telling people that snakes
will live forever
if they can learn to speak

I and the sky roam
the eroding and the die
the why all is just a dream
folding all ending destiny
like fading laundry

buds and toads and pale skies
roll the dice we know
there is a deep breath
only the earth can hear
a balance already spoken for

~

there are swinging doors
by the freedom calling
this side of looking at it

daring is no option
risking the rest of your days

is a matter of coping
with what moves forward
no more no less

there were anchors
dragging the bottom of the sea
blinking buoys floating
ringing over waves of water

there are still more days
golden straws to hold on to

there are old pale pubs
this side of memory lost
jeans bold and brash

I sound like a fool
bursting with images
at the very core of observance

~

stirred like a boiled mushroom
in a primordial soup
I in a dance with day and trees
find no way to tell you
why motion is so important

183

gross waves are men on the run
desserts full of scorpions
dying for recipes to make bombs

there are butterflies
that only live a few days

remedies are for the naked and the bald
routines are for the still sleeping
one can always be more
than the nature of day's order
being it all is one way

ancient vernal equinox
carrying fairy dreams and pixies
rolling with laughter
is just another dream we lost
nothing more

~

solemnity is just another word
for leaving importance behind
what come next is a matter opinion

tides broke like brittle porcelain
on streets dreaming of sand
there were no umbrellas

stereotypes do not walk out
leaving the sermon unattended
they will enforce the law

dreams are fake currency
as far as laughter go
in realms of too much brooding

dared into a different say so
I walked just to find you
enhancing my steps

dereliction and iron bars
is my only heritage
on a bridge across the unknown

~

stolen like a day on the run
fledged like a bird or a butterfly
by the motion of facing life
held like a newly hatched chick
in the palm of your hand

it's all about poetry
the way you search for words
in the rolling tide of I
in the slow breeze

above harbored water
rainbow-oily

there's a slow ticking in bushes
where sparrows congregate
in the cool of the afternoon
one thought can make a difference

stealth is a looking out for more
look out
there are men running
for more hot chocolate and ties
pointing to the loot

severity is a trick
invented by the men
you fat-feed everyday
with the sweat of your intent

there are villages
where memory is not far
from the living
once in such abundance

it's all about poetry
the way these words
finds your sullen heart
in a sudden flash

~

I've seen generation after generation
leap into the lushness of grass
rolling like green water
billowing like horizontal sails

there is just one wind left
to hold the memories
the air that once enclosed this body
keeps my form in a fading whisper

a viper down a heron left
the tide frames any man's gust or tirade
there are sailor-tales at the far end
of the taxman's liquid street

I've seen the best of us
die with the rest rolling but
grass is just grass
a wind is only a wave of air

~

lost in a pool of wild images
televised on the inside
of closed eye lids

totalled amongst the ones
never to return
from the sleep of drugs

one is always on the rise
from dark sanction quarrels
to a bright elevation

dare the next day then
fly the night with bright fish
sleeping in shoals

so many coming around
while the rest will die
for a glimpse of white water

derelict and forlorn
there are no further say so
amongst the unborn

wish you better will roll
with the best of our time
till I time will no more

rectified and wronged
all at the same time
motion has no legal parent

deemed and sold for tears
at the final market
will give you no credit

there is only this I
this one brittle breeze
in fickle ether

~

derelict and still with night
tenderly touching day's end
with a soft lamentation
skin still in greeting
the wind calls you by a name
I call so still with agreement
and no better

I a blue stranger like sky
diving into yesterday's echo
framed in pale colours
absolute no more
is always the wave in a formula
ale in a goblet of dreams

destined to wander wide out
to see dead men in silence
ruled by the slow flow
of tidal blood in vein

deemed for a day or so
on green summer night

I am a temporarily see
a why in a house of seasons
a not saying anything
that I cannot observe
deemed by fake reasons
and winds I do not own
to roll with the I time

~

dogs will finally lie down
stop running with the rest
of paws on sand
trickling down thin waists
of impossible presence

drool you daily fooled
redeem your chips
before tidal tomorrow
finds a way to skin you flat
in the riff raff mood of old age

the window is open
summer is ticking by again
panting in slow motion

for the sake of a poster
pinned to my sunny wall

funny people will not be night
or play classical guitar
lesser men always find a way

to diminish day's last glow
where worms rest in the I

steady now fellow laminators
let's all varnish the world together
for one more shine to go
with the rest of all there is to be
just to be of different

reek demon in lime and disguise
your money is not valid here
what your dark fire needs
is the evening of another day
when the living is not I

~

reek you vile I am not
and tonight is no difference
there is still so much to care for
in the orange of roof tiles
glistening with evening water

191

trees in green with any such summer
will still roll with twilight after twilight

I can hear whales singing
on the pond radio
am I a part of the congregation
daring slow worms and unwilling thistles
to dance with the rest of us
just for the sake of it

hollow is the price wired men
must reckon with
nightfall is a smooth curtain
kerosene is another way to laugh
when skulls rattle on chains
over water turning into vapour

I dreamed there was a slow fire
a luminosity turning I into night
into the coming of the flawed
I will not run for major tonight
pleading for more salt
I will not be silently safe

~

serendipity is a leaking facet
known to those
that queue

by the diving board
it is so frightening

one after the other
they all break the green surface
the cemetery grass
is semen falling in wet soil
swirling a rocky cove goodbye

after the first death
there are so many other
running is just a different way
to squeeze common letters
into numbers of no mystery

~

I will not face tomorrow
with a sad face
or a wish for jig saw puzzles

nor will I look for more
than any day can offer
when it comes to live jazz

relentlessly I drill the air
I find focus to be a virtue
putting I will be on my wall

dare me not I will not go
there are so many ways
to break a soft glance with the eye

perhaps once there were fairies
banshees wailing
today we have the radio

we are short of dreams
we hurry down running corridors
we do stop to say hello

there is no difference
between a pool of moonshine
and a soft goodbye

~

seamlessly floating above the reed
fish in a dreamless afternoon
lurk in a different fashion
dread is a Jamaican word
effortless runs with so many threads
one could tie knots forever
so many dire men queuing
for lost days to reappear
winding up yesterdays like lost candy
wrapped in all the colours

any mind might find
to be of a fulfilling kind

raptured into I am still dying
wired like an old gun
wrapped around the neck
timbered like a forest on trucks
running down the evolution of men
able to eat all the what's left

I see no future in politics
or letting the rich be in charge
there is no final solution
beyond the coming
into a different understanding
and still we must die

~

soft death fade into goodbye
delayed fractions of no more falling
pieces of reality coming together

adhesive to the very core
of keeping it all together

summer was a handful
candle lit lights
swung high above the blinking pool

a thin moon played the fool
with no sense of belonging

dire masters of the inevitable death
will pass and their children
will dance on graves
dug by the high inlet men
dug deep into sea view slopes

we are all a fall and a sneeze
a few steps in no specific direction
intention and a hope to go
a lot of hail Mary's
and rosaries on funeral pyres

cross my heart and hope
will never die of consideration
while I rescue immigrants
imminent and close at high sea
war is a mostly a poor man's tale

~

still face of the moon
falls in dark water supplies
where fish in adoration pray
for more days and more chips
at the roulette table

there is a difference
between a toad on a mission
and a wind lost amongst the trees
we need to reclaim the silence in the reed
the sound of birds in our instruments

straws of a tubular importance
line up expecting more rain
sonority is a young girl
breaking morning into chimes
dead people do not cry

scarred like a timpani on the run
or an oboe with the ambition
to rule all stray and ordinary days
with laws hastily put in place
I claim the moves on my chart

stranded filled danced and lied to
there is always another day to blame
there will always be a final silence

another I am the I that I am
and you will be the you of I when I go

here is music in the distance I
soft songs bleeding sky into darkness
weary men fall asleep in emergency rooms
there will be another day
where we can be a new story

it was a night before the fall
the dare walked unchallenged
through bleak halls of what not
the see through was a delusion

remembering the dream
I told myself that
it is of no importance why anyone
will choose the grassy knoll

there are wired thoughts
that can move trees
there are solitary men
capable of turning time to water

~

"wish me upon a star" she said
"bold me like a wave
waiting to come home"
she looked decided
and I rolled my own water
into the distance
there was a man selling pockets
another telling tales
of a species inhabiting the space
between our most sincere words

"rapt me" "let me hold your gun
just to make sure you will not aim
at the rest of continuance"
she was gone
I spent a whole afternoon
looking for her in winds and water
remembering her words
and I just had to go
where day turned summer to silt
were attempts to survive fail

~

still like a glider on silent winds
a bird with no sense of position
a longing to live full beak and eye

derelict like a boulder forgotten
deep below the farmer's soil
I move one year at the time

stipulated like a dark tree
waiting for the coming storm
where you will be the wind

rapture is a sign of insanity
rolling chaos like speed heads
down avenues of pale death

199

the height is of no importance
nor the way lullabies tilt
high above the smoky surf

I am the binder of soft tools
the bender of ways
the sweeper of anyone's chimney

~

streamed into thin horizontal lines
ocean greyhounds finally set sail
into the very next day

hordes of the newly bred
run for cover
like baby toads at midsummer
the moon is full for three days

whispered into tomorrow
three men on the lake long for new oars
for a new semantic discourse

when the I is no more
I will not be there
to defend all that I was

~

dogs bark fiercely
at brittle boned afternoon tea
rolling dreaded daylight
into rainbow spliffs
with the dead and the thunder
gone into yesterday gone
a rift lost in dreams

a burst of suddenness
in the brevity of motion
leaves men busy sweating
in dark engine-rooms
where go fast into days dying
to the sound of driftwood
is a way to softly break

~

parked in a garden with bees
I dare to finalize the rocky torso
turning rain in late August
there is no relevant lament to go

pierced like a lobe or a lip at sea
rolled into bleak tomorrow

I cannot find any more to say
than translucent is my air

gargoyled and weathered
like a headstone on high wire
I dream my options into slow night
no one will survive

~

I looked and looked again
there was no solid me to be found
pans and pots dangled
on the threshold of no more

I need to break a few eggs
rotate anticlockwise
rub the other cheek with oil
from camomile and thyme
drool like a fierce fiend
just because I totally disagree
turn my hand into a wind
set fire to the icons

passion is a false dream
rolling bones into a different matter
backdating direness into a tomorrow

where I will leave all messages
unheard unanswered and totally ignored

~

do not worry little cloud
full of hands chiming at late night
be sure to fold your memories
like winds on the run tend to do
there will be no final reckoning
no time for a bed roll

I saw men riding dead hard-ons
all the way to the bickering bank
sisters begging for more money
the two-faced dared
balmy air tubs to run
for yet another beach front
money never fails to burn
ceremonious tables at nightfall
run a duck entertains the darkness
with the striped and the old
with a no certain marrow evening
for the jackdaw to sing
the rest into the void into dark

seamless like air rounding
an old bag of crisps
one is a fall into no good

I dreamed once I could fly
high above a coniferous forest
making speed with my hands

today all is fenced up
and blue skies are for sale
on a market to die for

~

sultry sunday on the rebound
steepled and died for
so many times
in aisles of stale ceremony

run child run
there are collars on the prowl
collecting all one wind can muster

I see poor men folding waves
mending speed with their hands
just to keep busy

day turns into more fish
wine flow freely
trees on the run congregate
music is admonished with water

pools of liquid knives roll
with a watery punch

hidden in days of sweet talk
there are men hoisting dark flags
others bind books for the blind
there are so many shadows

~

they congregate in visons
of blood that will not coagulate
they dare the rest of it
to follow dark suit

it is a mad input indeed
that comes with the territory
often dire men in the I condition
lean towards the blame

solemn and so tired
one I is more than enough

to drive a silvery nail
through the wet canopy

scratched dumped and
left for dead

the flourishing abides
in temple-times of furtherness

one man is not enough
to strike a final blow
two might play checkers
into the falling night

~

there are laps to be found
running like rivers
at the bottom of all say so

who cares will find reception
in the flames of a hot Wi-Fi
doing connection

I will not park this poem here
I will not pay for a ticket
that will take me nowhere

perhaps you can see me
perhaps it is only I
from the beginning

~

solitary men cry for more fish
in parks where young mothers
dangle limbs pointing
to the certainty of it all ending
there's no day like today

rolled into yesterday's joints
moved by chords of dry leaves
there is no need to foresee
a different way
to meet the coming of darkness

ramified into a billion suns
racing through the dark longing
of being one step closer
to the incubated sleep of books
I am still unread humming

redeemed it seemed to one man
stripped into pale skin leaking
fluids of unfulfillment

amongst the children laughing
into the die another day

~

wish me suns and stars
an ivory smiles at the end
of any blue given day

rosaries held tight
backwaters overflowing
there is no redemption

sold by the fire of mischief
one told the other
the secrete of trees in adoration

there's going to be a full moon
at the end of this week
the green will not bend

ceremonies turn day to dark
men will still march for the sake
of more shields and shoes

wish me suns and stars
a bottle of old imaged serum
eyes opening to the flowers

~

do not celebrate tungsten
though it will boil last
and is essential to
any living organism

do not party for the sake
of more iridium
too dense to catch a fire

more beer is needed to the suburbs
more lustful men
hoisting flags of surrender
there is a wanted station
just beyond the second thought
where rhythm guitars
find solace in the inexplicable

~

it's all about the weed
the speed of perception
the layers upon layers
of straddled reality falling
unfolding remoulding
scaffolding reaching
for modest time
to warp between the eyes
of the ones imbibed
inhaled rolled into carpets
from the far east

in the end it will be said
one man died on a Saturday

another pleaded with night
just to get ahead
there are moles in the clockwork
red sand in old bottles
remarkable futures that end
fish that jump
gargoyled and silent
in streams of other men

~

better men dance in those streams
stung by creatures of no evil
randomly intercepted by pillars
falling like an old Greek rain
over fields of wild camomile

senators of inhaled religion
prohibitors of holy intake
rainmakers with bills and coins
etched on the retinas
will all melt at sundown

jars of incompetence roll
like dead wishes going nowhere
serpents of male religion

skulk in left over shadows
expecting to score

there such calamity
in the continuation
men that will kill to get ahead
days that will arise
in times of fear

~

the flawless will not inherit
the morons will not be counted
when sundown goes nuclear
silly atomic heart mother
is just another way
to immortalise matter

Casper put an end to Judy
with a sack of black beans
no sudden imbued rush
could ever substitute
the what's going on
lusting for another well-done rib
lost in translation

the saturated glared
the meek
collected the refundable

it's just another night
undressed and out of place
where the dire ones
burn punch cards
and demand another go
at the table of more

~

summon me not dancing
below the dark sky of my heart
sing me not at early dawn
where no one man
can draw a jagged line
between the fading goners
and the silence in turn

there are ceremonies
where the old boot
is soft skinned and in love
smelling of vanilla and
all that comes
with any wished beginning
listed at day's yearning

spilled – lost in so many days
one foot deeply rooted
in the spoils of our fathers
I watch the passing hour

I will not go between
iced end and bright grace
for the sake of I have to

bitter drinks fall in river bars
where I is a lost concept
and the rest
like rotten vanilla
blends with the forlorn
that run with the rest of us

steepled I know
crammed into a jar of nothing
slept through
like a calf bereaved
danced through a nest of hornets
just to meet pure odium
at the gargoyled gate

so thoroughly boned to the eye
I – a fish in the sun
ready and sought for by the poor
and the meek eyed infidels
find life in a glass of water absurd
where I as it were found another you
to bind my roundabout motion
to a rebel nosed cause

framed solicited and wired
I – the stringency
low figures find tamed –
walk estranged I
rolling daily papers
into a furnace on the run
I feign custody just to be alive
under boughs of silver

~

I am the unsolicited one
the unwanted – the meek
old man by default
the one crying for ends
lost in the mystery of music
for fettered circumstances
fed by the hour of reckoning
lost in the hall

the illusion of redemption
is such an easy way out
– suckle and die –
there's always new hardware
claiming attention
by the rest of your days
the humus is finally exuded
in a hot aspiration

~

ominous into the verbal
the herbal the frivolous roll
across the circus floor
I it seems do not walk gently
nor read my timed future
in tea leaves or yarrow sticks

serendipity is a fox trot
a night at the Cavern
so many years ago
before noon was a matter
of getting your shit together
with cast iron lampposts on the run

sold out will not matter
when dark rain is in reverse
time is a bright badge brigade on the run
facing inevitable erasure in movies
made for one last jump
on the trampoline

~

there are but a few of us left
that will not instigate or ignite

random fires of supremacy
just for the hell of it

men of the cloth drool
at the thought of nursery crimes
dead from the foot up
they see no need for leniency

charcoaled into dark night
where visions of soft skin
call for more wine
one needs to be embraced

random selections boom
like erupting death
I only see you beloved
walking by my side

~

who am I to dispute the fact
that I am you too
that I too
roll like dark thunder
between worlds scolded by light
never perceived nor called for
by other here entities than I
and I running
insisting on prevalence

grass rolled into green dragons
fuming at the I door slamming
on the way out to nowhere
Ramses will not interrupt
nor will the incarnations
of human void and silence
tender wistfulness
is all that is left
there is no river to die for

~

one man whispered I
into the falling night

another rode dark tears
all the way to the bank

there's a blue man
smiling in shiny armour
soldered by pain and power
over years and years

one man begged for more
the towering thief in him
lurked behind the tone
of his own voice

~

who am I one man dangling
above one world and its void
derelict to the very bone
of conceit and misconception
redeemed by water and clocks

serendipity holds no sway here
where continuity is a matter
of keeping your legs crossed
never delving into the other I
where sureness is theft

steamed into times of watery waves
I keep falling into traps
of induced anaesthesia rolling
like thunder at mute movie theatres
caught dying off guard

your mother is my mother
your time is also a foul lottery
kneaded by celestial bakers
at the end of the green lime light
running from every station

I see you at the end game
unfolding fires of no good
doing their nasty thing

dealing and sealing a grift
dissolving in a no good will

wishful dances above the surf
will not change the code
we are here and we are here
because it is what we are
at the end of the day

~

walked into near oblivion
I was talked into turning the lights off
before night rolled into day again

herb remedies do not apply here
nor will tight rope umbrellas be needed
the pointless are still pointless

the rescue team turned up at eleven
there was still smoke smouldering
from badly burned carcasses

if you can hear a soft hum on the radio
a voice in defiance shredding ties
it's I turning day into spinal wine

sumptuous worried
solid as far as clinging goes
I dare the rest without fear

~

I read the sky today
bricks and mortar ready
for the big leap

once there was a bird
chirping at the kitchen knife
turning sun into water

reflections bother me
tiled into uneasy comfort
above the charcoal trees

~

timed into trickle and trench
bedded by famed fires and raw intellect
running wild with tell-tales of I can
whispered around late evening ears
fastened to kitchen walls like flies
constantly cooking dinner for three

derelict in drops of water
in unpredicted stories
yet retold all over for amber and I
we're late-night fires
telling our side of the story

we run with the mixed crowd
we break all intention
I sitar and I tabla has gone to fruit
a rambling of sorts
roll I echoes into solar plus I

day is teeming life
yearning and intense
all life is here
breathing
growing moving

all will face death
all will dance with skulls
all will rattle
rattle

this is what we are

~

the ex-filed are gathering their say-so
telling tales of their own

sending letters to the red queen
taking all kinds of pills

I am a mindless butterfly
facing the one day I have
with a caterpillar smile to go
with fake sumptuousness

~

timed and timed again
I – rolled into last ocean I darkness –
fought for by the run for it

I infidel in season can still be I
not ruled by laws of odium or love
or the selfish the small in eye

mirrors glued to the wall
will not matter
I find no peace here
where the living is in retreat

this old country is elegy only
songs are constantly lost
amongst the foothills
where forests carry old scars

gasping rivers and green diversity lost
lost to the highest bidder
god planners skulk in trenches

he who pleads right of interpretation
is an I infidel and I will not hear
the echo of circumcised dreams in demise

About the Author

Bengt O Björklund left his native Sweden to seek his hippie dreams in 1968, but ended up in a Turkish prison for possession of a small amount of hashish. A portion of this story was creatively represented in the movie *Midnight Express*. His time in this prison was spent with several other artists of various disciplines who had also been imprisoned for cultural or political reasons. During this time Bengt wrote his first poems and songs and also began painting. In 1973 Bengt was transferred to a Swedish prison where he continued to paint and write. After his release he resettled in his homeland and began to paint and write, play music and perform his work. He also emigrated, first to the UK, the to Brazil in 1983. 1990 he returned to Sweden.

Bengt is the author of many books. He writes fluently in both Swedish and English. This is the third poetry collection of his English poetry. In 2017, a short biopic film, My Moon, was made which chronicled his early years and the years he spent in a Turkish prison which served as the impetus for his later creative life. The film was first shown at the Oberhausen International Short Film Festival in May 2018. Just prior to the release of this first edition, Bengt was named the Sweden Beat Poet Laureate by the Beat Poetry Foundation.

Middle Creek Publishing Titles

MIDDLE CREEK

PUBLISHING

www.ingramcontent.com/pod-product-compliance
Lightning Source LLC
Chambersburg PA
CBHW070348090426
42733CB00009B/1326